Economic Factors in the Growth of Corporation Giving

Economic Factors in the Growth of Corporation Giving

RALPH L. NELSON

Queens College, City University of New York

National Bureau of Economic Research
Occasional Paper 111

Published by the NATIONAL BUREAU OF ECONOMIC
RESEARCH and RUSSELL SAGE FOUNDATION
NEW YORK   1970

Standard Book Number 87154–615–9

© 1970 by the NATIONAL BUREAU OF ECONOMIC RESEARCH and RUSSELL SAGE FOUNDATION

Printed in the United States of America
Library of Congress Catalog Card Number: 70–104182

RELATION OF THE DIRECTORS
TO THE WORK AND PUBLICATIONS
OF THE NATIONAL BUREAU OF ECONOMIC RESEARCH

1. The object of the National Bureau of Economic Research is to ascertain and to present to the public important economic facts and their interpretation in a scientific and impartial manner. The Board of Directors is charged with the responsibility of ensuring that the work of the National Bureau is carried on in strict conformity with this object.

2. The President of the National Bureau shall submit to the Board of Directors, or to its Executive Committee, for their formal adoption all specific proposals for research to be instituted.

3. No research report shall be published until the President shall have submitted to each member of the Board the manuscript proposed for publication, and such information as will, in his opinion and in the opinion of the author, serve to determine the suitability of the report for publication in accordance with the principles of the National Bureau. Each manuscript shall contain a summary drawing attention to the nature and treatment of the problem studied, the character of the data and their utilization in the report, and the main conclusions reached.

4. For each manuscript so submitted, a special committee of the Board shall be appointed by majority agreement of the President and Vice Presidents (or by the Executive Committee in case of inability to decide on the part of the President and Vice Presidents), consisting of three directors selected as nearly as may be one from each general division of the Board. The names of the special manuscript committee shall be stated to each Director when the manuscript is submitted to him. It shall be the duty of each member of the special manuscript committee to read the manuscript. If each member of the manuscript committee signifies his approval within thirty days of the transmittal of the manuscript, the report may be published. If at the end of that period any member of the manuscript committee withholds his approval, the President shall then notify each member of the Board, requesting approval or disapproval of publication, and thirty days additional shall be granted for this purpose. The manuscript shall then not be published unless at least a majority of the entire Board who shall have voted on the proposal within the time fixed for the receipt of votes shall have approved.

5. No manuscript may be published, though approved by each member of the special manuscript committee, until forty-five days have elapsed from the transmittal of the report in manuscript form. The interval is allowed for the receipt of any memorandum of dissent or reservation, together with a brief statement of his reasons, that any member may wish to express; and such memorandum of dissent or reservation shall be published with the manuscript if he so desires. Publication does not, however, imply that each member of the Board has read the manuscript, or that either members of the Board in general or the special committee have passed on its validity in every detail.

6. Publications of the National Bureau issued for informational purposes concerning the work of the Bureau and its staff, or issued to inform the public of activities of Bureau staff, and volumes issued as a result of various conferences involving the National Bureau shall contain a specific disclaimer noting that such publication has not passed through the normal review procedures required in this resolution. The Executive Committee of the Board is charged with review of all such publications from time to time to ensure that they do not take on the character of formal research reports of the National Bureau, requiring formal Board approval.

7. Unless otherwise determined by the Board or exempted by the terms of paragraph 6, a copy of this resolution shall be printed in each National Bureau publication.

(*Resolution adopted October 25, 1926 and revised February 6, 1933, February 24, 1941, and April 20, 1968*)

ADVISORY COMMITTEE ON THE PHILANTHROPY STUDY

In the planning and review of its studies of the role of philanthropy in the American economy, the National Bureau has benefited from the advice and guidance of this committee. The committee's concurrence with the views expressed in this report, however, is not to be assumed. The members of the committee are:

F. Emerson Andrews, *Foundation Library Center, retired*
Gary S. Becker, *Columbia University*
Merle Curti, *University of Wisconsin*
Richard Eells, *Columbia University*
Lyman Ford, *United Community Funds and Councils of America*
Raymond W. Goldsmith, *Yale University*
Covington Hardee, *Clark Carr and Ellis*
Rembrandt C. Hiller, Jr., *Sears Roebuck and Company*
Thomas Karter, *Social Security Administration*
Herbert E. Klarman, *State University of New York*
Ray M. Peterson, *Equitable Life Assurance Society, retired*
John A. Pollard, *Council for Financial Aid to Education, deceased*
W. Homer Turner, *United States Steel Foundation*
Walter M. Upchurch, Jr., *Shell Companies Foundation*
Donald Young, *Rockefeller University*

to
DAVID
and
RACHEL

ACKNOWLEDGMENTS

THIS STUDY represents part of the research on the role of philanthropy in the American economy conducted by the National Bureau of Economic Research under a grant from Russell Sage Foundation. This support, reflecting the Foundation's long standing interest in improving our knowledge about, and the effectiveness of, private philanthropy, is most gratefully acknowledged.

The research has benefited from the assistance of a number of persons. In the early stages of the study discussions with the late Frank G. Dickinson, with whom responsibility for the over-all project was divided, helped to lay the groundwork for the research plan. At various stages Natalie Naylor, Rosanne Cole, and Cynthia Norris served as capable research assistants. The editorial skills of Joan Tron added much to the style and clarity of the manuscript. The craftsmanship of H. Irving Forman is apparent in the charts.

The manuscript received very thorough readings from the staff reading committee of Solomon Fabricant and Jacob Mincer. Their comments led to improvements ranging over the whole work. Fabricant read the whole manuscript in several of its revisions. His sustained involvement and interest led me to re-evaluate, and frequently change, its organization and a number of basic conceptual treatments. The result, thanks to him, is one in which I feel much more satisfaction. Mincer and Yoel Haitovsky were of particular assistance in the design and interpretation of the statistical analysis.

Thanks are due the members of the National Bureau's Directors Reading Committee, Erwin D. Canham, Crawford H. Greenewalt, and Willard L. Thorp. Mr. Thorp gave the manuscript a very thorough reading, as did F. Emerson Andrews, Foundation Library Center (*retired*) and John H. Watson III, National Industrial Conference Board. Their penetrating comments, covering every part of the study, added much to its precision and balance.

Thanks are due the research directors of the National Bureau for their forbearance at interruptions in the progress of the study. This was particularly manifest midway in the research when I was generously permitted to postpone work on the Bureau project to undertake and complete a Russell Sage Foundation study of the investment policies of foundations.

A final word of thanks is due my wife, Ann, for her encouragement, patience, and, perhaps most important of all in the uncertain business of research, a much valued sense of perspective.

RALPH L. NELSON

CONTENTS

TABLES AND CHARTS

Appendix Tables

Charts

Economic Factors in the Growth of Corporation Giving

ONE
꒦꒦꒦

Introduction
and Summary

In 1964, business corporations in the United States reported $729 million in gifts and contributions on their income tax returns. In that year the gross national product was $629 billion. This meant that, of every $1,000 spent by all purchasers of goods and services in the country, $1.16 was used to support the recipients of corporate philanthropy. These recipients, in turn, used these contributions to provide society with health and welfare services totaling about $320 million, educational services totaling about $280 million, civic and cultural services totaling about $40 million, and other philanthropic services totaling about $90 million.

The growth in giving from the pre-Depression period has been large. For 1929, like 1964 a year of high levels of corporate activity, corporation giving has been estimated at $22 to $32 million.[1] In 1929, only $0.21 to $0.31 of every $1,000 spent in the country was used for corporate philanthropy, compared with the $1.16 of 1964.

Direct and comprehensive data on corporation giving begin in 1936, when contributions were first reportable on corporation income tax returns and so entered the statistical tabulations of the Internal Revenue Service. For this reason this study examines in detail the growth in giving from 1936 through 1964, the most recent year for which data are presently available.

ORIENTATION OF THE STUDY

The purpose of this study is to examine the growth of corporate giving and, insofar as possible, to measure the separate effects of

---

[1] F. Emerson Andrews, *Corporation Giving* (New York: Russell Sage Foundation, 1952), p. 35, and U.S. Department of Commerce, *U.S. Income and Output, A Supplement to the Survey of Current Business* (Washington: 1958), Table 1–12, pp. 134–135.

1

changes in corporate attitudes and giving behavior and of developments of a more strictly economic character. Changes in corporate attitudes toward giving reflect changes in the role of the business corporation not only as an economic unit but also as a social institution shaped by noneconomic forces. In the literature, increasing attention has been paid to the complex noneconomic role that the corporation—particularly the large corporation—plays in the broader society. The corporation is viewed as a citizen responsible to its several constituencies of employees, shareholders, customers, suppliers, government, and general society. In these discussions, philanthropic giving has figured prominently.[2]

The changing institutional basis for greater giving has been accompanied, and perhaps encouraged, by liberalization of the legal right of corporations to make contributions. Such liberalization has affected not only the amount of contributions, but their diversity, as contributions have shifted, in part, from those of demonstrable, direct, and immediate benefit to the corporation to those that confer a more uncertain, indirect, and deferred benefit. Such legal and institutional developments are reviewed in greater detail in Chapter Three.

Changes in the legal and attitudinal bases for corporate giving have taken place concurrently with a number of important economic developments, which have also played a significant role in the growth of giving. The effects of these economic developments have been strong and will be measured so that the role of noneconomic factors may be gauged with some degree of precision. Over the quarter-century from the late 1930's to the early 1960's, there were great changes in the economy, changes affecting the business corporation as an engine of production, an earner of profits, and a taxpayer. The gross national product rose from $87.0 to $560.4 billion a year during this period. Before-tax profits, for corporations with net income, rose from $8.8 to $59.0 billion a year. The net after-tax cost of tax-deductible contributions declined as marginal tax rates on corporate income rose from 15 to 19 to 38 to 52 per cent. The tax rate increase was accelerated during two wartime periods of excess-profits taxes. In the

---

[2] See, e.g., Richard Eells, *Corporation Giving in a Free Society* (New York: Harper & Bros., 1956; W. Homer Turner, "The Emerging Pattern of Corporation Philanthropy," Management Seminars on Company Contributions, Princeton, New Jersey, October 16, 1956, and October 29, 1957; Covington Hardee, "Philanthropy and the Business Corporation, Existing Guidelines—Future Policy," in Frank G. Dickinson, Editor, *Philanthropy and Public Policy* (New York: National Bureau of Economic Research, 1962).

first of these, the maximum rate reached 91 per cent, and, in the second, 82 per cent. After-tax profits, for corporations with net income, rose from $7.7 to $36.9 billion a year.

The growth and proliferation of company-sponsored foundations may have affected the trend in contributions. Although such foundations typically serve as pass-through devices, to facilitate the administration of corporate contributions programs, some have been built into substantial endowments. Where this has occurred, the timing and size of the contributions flows have been affected. Some measurement of the size of this effect will be attempted in the final chapter of this book.

UNRECORDED PHILANTHROPIC INVOLVEMENT

In this study, the descriptions and analysis have, of necessity, been based mostly on tax return data. It should be noted, however, that the dollar amounts of contributions reported on tax returns understate the size of corporate philanthropic involvement, possibly by a considerable amount. One important element in corporate philanthropy not reflected in the tax return data is the value of the services of corporate officers in fund-raising and other charitable activities. Much of this is done on "company time" and is regarded as a normal and, indeed, an expected part of a manager's corporate duties. These activities, therefore, are as much a part of the corporation's explicit commitment to philanthropy as is its budget for cash contributions. Nor does the contributions budget always fully measure the size of a corporation's cash outlays for philanthropy. Expenditures having significant elements of philanthropic motivation and effect, but which also contain an even greater element of ordinary business motivation and effect, are likely to be reported as business expenses. The valuation and accounting treatment of gifts in kind may also lead to an understatement of corporation giving or, under certain circumstances, to an overstatement.[3] In interpreting the findings of the study, these data limitations should be kept in mind.[4]

---

[3] See Orace Johnson, "Corporate Giving: A Note on Profit Maximization and Accounting Disclosure," *Journal of Accounting Research*, Spring, 1965, pp. 75–85.

[4] A related corporate commitment to philanthropy is the handling of employees' contributions to charitable activities. Corporate resources thus occupied are usually not included in contributions budgets. The contributions of employees are classified as personal and, of course, do not appear in the statistics of corporation giving.

SUMMARY OF FINDINGS

The Growth of Corporation Giving

Chapter Two describes in detail the growth in giving from the late 1930's to the early 1960's. Over this period, reported corporation giving grew from an annual rate of $31 million to $595 million. Relative to total economic activity, as measured by the gross national product, its share increased threefold, from one-thirtieth of 1 per cent in 1936–1940 to one-tenth of 1 per cent in the period 1960–1964. The increase in share was not a gradual one, however; rather it took place in the four war years 1940 to 1944. Since 1944 the share has moved within a relatively narrow range about one-tenth of 1 per cent.

Measured against corporate net income or profits, the observed growth pattern departed significantly from that measured against national product. Gifts as a percentage of income rose sharply during World War II. However, the two postwar decades witnessed not merely a maintenance of the historically high percentage then achieved but a growth to much higher levels.

Corporate net income was chosen as the base for most comparisons of giving ratios for several reasons. First, income represents a tolerably useful measure of the scale of corporate activity. Second, income has direct operational significance in the giving decision. Corporate income is the only legal source of funds from which contributions may be drawn. Careful distinctions are made by corporations between distributions of capital as against income, and the prior claims of creditors and owners in the distribution of the corporation's capital are subject to detailed safeguards. In addition, the net income basis is recognized in the Internal Revenue Code requirement that not more than 5 per cent of income may be deducted as contributions in determining taxable income.[5]

---

[5] In relating contributions to corporate net income, the record for only those corporations reporting a positive net income will be summarized. Corporations with positive net income accounted for 98.6 per cent of total contributions over the period, and so the loss in coverage from excluding corporations with losses is small. It is more than compensated for by the gain in comparability of giving-to-income percentages that are free from the fluctuations produced by period-to-period variations in the loss experience of corporations.

A comparison of the trend in giving-to-income percentages for all corporations and for net-income corporations is provided in Orace Johnson "Corporate Philanthropy: An Analysis of Corporate Contributions," *Journal of Business*, October, 1966, Figure 1, p. 493. This chart shows that, while the levels of the two series differ, the slopes of trend lines fitted to the series would be very close to one another, and no systematic divergence over the period is indicated.

The trend in corporate giving as a percentage of corporate income and of the national product is summarized in Table 1. Column 2 shows that, aside from the 1950–1953 Korean War period, corporate givings' share of the gross national product rose only slightly from 1946–1949 through the years 1960 to 1964. By contrast, columns 3, 4, and 5 show that corporate giving rose markedly as a percentage of corporate income (variously defined). Columns 6 and 8 reconcile the large increase in share of net income with the slight increase in share of national product. They show that both before- and after-tax corporate income, as a percentage of gross national product, declined from 1946–1949 through 1960–1964. Had corporate contributions merely been maintained at the same percentage of corporate income, their share of gross national product would have been lower by a factor of about one-third.

The patterns for the World War II and the Korean War periods deserve separate comment. As shown in Table 1, very high corporate income and excess-profits tax rates and very high levels of contributions were evident in both periods. Both were characterized by ratios of contributions to disposable income that rose significantly above the trend. This pattern is examined in more detail in Chapter Two.

The percentage of income remaining after the payment of income taxes declined considerably over the period, reflecting the rise in tax rates (*column 7*). Corporate contributions, averaging less than 1 per cent of before-tax income, could have done little to offset this decline, even considering the fact that an increasing proportion of contributions was "paid for" by the government through tax deductibility.[6] On this construction, after-tax income was taken as the more meaningful measure of corporate ability to make contributions.[7]

As a percentage of corporate income before taxes the growth in giving was substantial, the percentage in the period 1960–1964 being more than three times that of 1936–1940 (1.00 compared with 0.31 per cent). Measured relative to after-tax income, the increase was of course much greater. In 1960–1964, gifts as a percentage of after-tax income (*columns 4 and 5*) were about four and one-half times those

---

[6] Tax deductibility, of course, did play a role in the growth of giving over a period of rising tax rates. Its effect on the net after-tax cost of contributions is treated separately, and is summarized below.

[7] Giving is expressed as percentage of after-tax income defined in two ways: before contributions and after contributions (*see note b to Table 1*). Although the former, in concept, is more fully the equivalent of corporate disposable income, the distinction makes little difference in the empirical description of trends. See also Appendix Table II.

TABLE 1   Relation of Corporate Gifts and Contributions to Gross National Product, Corporate Before-Tax Income, and Corporate After-Tax Income, 1936–1964, by Subperiod[a]

		Gifts and Contributions as Percentage of					Corporate Net Income After Taxes, Before Gifts and Contributions, as Percentage of	
Period	Average Annual Reported Contributions (Millions of 1936 dollars) (1)	Gross National Product (2)	Corporate Net Income Before Taxes (3)	Corporate Net Income After Taxes, Before Gifts and Contributions[b] (4)	Corporate Net Income After Taxes, After Gifts and Contributions (5)	Corporate Net Income Before Taxes as Percentage of GNP (6)	Before-Tax Income (7)	GNP (8)
1936–40	$ 28	0.032	0.310	0.363	0.364	10.43	85.5	8.92
1941–45	121	0.088	0.645	1.275	1.280	13.63	50.6	6.89
1946–49	129	0.095	0.709	1.032	1.038	13.43	68.7	9.23
1950–53	183	0.111	0.848	1.503	1.511	13.10	56.4	7.38
1954–59	178	0.094	0.833	1.388	1.397	11.26	60.0	6.76
1960–64	237	0.105	0.998	1.584	1.597	10.50	63.0	6.62

[a] Based on constant (1936) dollar data aggregated for given time periods.
[b] Computed by adding to corporate net income after taxes, after gifts and contributions (as presented in the U.S. Treasury Department's *Statistics of Income, Corporation Income Tax Returns*, for the several years), an estimate of the net after-tax cost of reported gifts and contributions. These estimates are presented in Appendix Tables II and III.

TABLE 2 After-Tax Net Cost of Gifts and Contributions as Percentage of Corporate Net Income After Taxes, Corporations with Net Incomes, 1936–1964, by Subperiod (Dollar values in millions of 1936 dollars)

Total for Years	Gifts and Contributions (1)	Average Price[a] of $1 in Contributions for Period (2)	Estimated Net After-Tax Cost of Gifts and Contributions (3)	Corporate Net Income After Taxes, Before Gifts and Contributions (4)	Column 3 as Percentage of Column 4 (5)
1936–40	$ 141.9	$0.77	$109	$39,115	0.28
1941–45	606.8	0.27	164	47,588	0.34
1946–49	516.7	0.59	306	50,091	0.61
1950–53	733.9	0.36	265	48,825	0.54
1954–59	1,069.9	0.48	515	77,081	0.67
1960–64	1,184.0	0.48	573	74,732	0.77

[a] Complement of the weighted average marginal tax rate paid by corporations accounting for the preponderance of contributions.

for 1936–1940, rising from 0.36 to 1.60 per cent. Also of significance has been the sustained increase over the period since World War II. From 1946–1949 to 1960–1964, giving as a percentage of after-tax income increased by 54 per cent, from 1.04 to 1.60 per cent.

The rise in contributions as a percentage of after-tax income did not mean that their net cost to corporations rose in the same proportion. Over the period the marginal tax rate on corporate income rose from an average of 23 per cent in 1936–1940 to 52 per cent in 1960–1964. Because of the deductibility of contributions, the net after-tax cost of one dollar in contributions declined by almost two-fifths over the period (*Table 2, column 2*). An important part of the growth thus represents an increase in the share of total contributions that has been absorbed by the general public, as represented by the tax collector, over a period of rising tax rates. The 1960–1964 gross flow of contributions was 8.3 times that of 1936–1940.[8] The growth in the net after-tax cost of these flows was considerably smaller: the average for 1960–1964 was only 5.3 times that of 1936–1940.

A much larger part of the growth in contributions represents an increase in the share of after-tax income that corporations have chosen to be out of pocket in their distributions to philanthropy. This may be seen in column 5 of Table 2, which shows that, as a percentage of the after-tax income base for giving, the after-tax cost of their

---

[8] In dollars of constant (1936) value.

reported philanthropic distributions rose from 0.28 per cent in 1936–1940 to 0.77 per cent in 1960–1964. Expressed in different terms, the growth in "real sacrifice" might be described as follows: Had corporations chosen to make the same out-of-pocket outlays relative to disposable income in 1960–1964 as they had in 1936–1940 (0.28 per cent), they would have made only 36 per cent of the gifts and contributions that they actually reported for 1960–1964. Instead of an average of $589 million per year, in current dollars, they would have contributed only about $212 million per year.

Chapter Three examines some of the factors that might account for the rise in giving described in Chapter Two. First there is analysis of the relationships between giving and possible causal economic factors, as revealed by their behavior over time. Then there is an analysis of cross-sectional data. In both analyses the technique of multiple correlation is used to identify the several relationships.

Economic Determinants of Giving

Three principal factors in giving were distinguished and an attempt was made, using time-series data, to measure their separate effects. The first was the net income of corporations, taken as the most relevant available measure of the scale of corporate activity. The second was the net after-tax cost or "price" of a given dollar amount of contributions. The third was the group of other factors that affect giving, of which the giving propensity of corporations is presumably the major component.

It was hypothesized that, with price and giving propensity held constant, contributions should bear a proportionate relationship to the scale of corporate activities over time. A priori, few reasons could be found for expecting that the growth in the scale of corporate activity, taken alone, would result in either a less than or more than proportionate growth in giving. The hypothesis thus predicts a scale elasticity of giving of one. The multiple regression analysis supports this hypothesis, with measured scale elasticities exhibiting values close to unity.

An attempt was made, going beyond the preceding hypothesis, to measure the effect on giving of the percentage rate of return on shareholders investment. This was done by including net worth as a variable in the multiple correlation analysis. Because income and rate of return were highly intercorrelated, it was difficult to separate neatly the scale and rate of return effects. The findings, although thus subject to a considerable degree of qualification, nonetheless suggested that the short-run responsiveness to changes in percentage rate of return was not large. The findings of the cross-sectional analysis, as reported below, also suggested a relatively low elasticity with respect to this variable. This is probably to be expected. Corporations might regard years of unusually high or low rates of return on investment as essentially temporary, and not significant enough to warrant a fully compensating adjustment in contributions.

Changes in corporate tax rates over the period meant that the net after-tax cost or "price" of a given dollar amount of contributions was subject to corresponding changes. Contributions serve to create a favorable public image of the corporation, and to encourage a social and political environment conducive to its survival and prosperity. As such they are properly regarded as one of the profit-enhancing inputs to the corporation, and their use might be determined by the same principles that determine the use of other such inputs. However, their benefits in this respect are more uncertain and often much longer deferred than that of other inputs. As a result, the immediate and certain tax savings that accompany contributions may weigh more heavily in a corporation's contributions decision.

In the regression analysis, the variable used to measure the tax effect was the complement of the marginal tax rate. This could be viewed as the "price" of, say, one dollar in contributions. The observed response of contributions to changes in tax rates (i.e., "price") produced elasticity coefficients that ranged around -1.0. This finding suggests that tax rate changes, and corresponding changes in the immediate and certain tax savings that accompany contributions, were an important factor in explaining the variation in giving.

The influence of long-run changes in other factors was the third element in the time-series analysis. The most apparent of these other factors was probably an increase in corporate propensity to give. Public pronouncements on the issue, as well as relaxations of legal restrictions over the period, suggested that corporations had become progressively more receptive to the notion that they should make contributions. To determine whether such apparent changes in underlying conditions were accompanied by a corresponding change in behavior, a trend variable (in effect, the equivalent of a secular or long-run residual factor) was included in the analysis. This was taken as a proxy for the change in the propensity to give, as well as for progressive changes in any other factors that might have influenced giving.

In the multiple regression analysis, the trend variable exhibited consistently high and significant values. This suggested that developments associated with the passage of time, other than scale and price, made an important independent contribution to the growth in giving. Although the trend variable could reflect progressive changes in factors other than the propensity of corporations to make contributions, no other factor presented itself as likely to have had as important an effect.

As an independent test of the effects of some of the factors examined in the time-series analysis, and to measure the effects of other factors, cross-sectional data were also examined. With changes over time removed from the analysis, the effects of such time-related factors as changes in tax rates and giving propensities could not be tested. However, the cross-sectional analysis permitted measurement of the relationship between giving and corporate size (measured by net assets as well as income), rate of return on investment, and the importance of labor versus capital in production.

The relationship between the size of a corporation and the amount of its contributions was examined first. It will be recalled that the estimated scale elasticity of giving was found to be about one. The implication was that size of corporate activities was proportionate in its effect on the percentage of income given. The cross-sectional analysis supported this finding, also producing scale elasticities close to one.

The degree to which a corporation employed people, as contrasted to capital, also appeared to have an important influence on the percentage of income given. This is probably not surprising, as much of corporation giving is employee-related. Contributions to local health and welfare drives are often based on the number of the company's employees in the community. College scholarship grants and matching grants to employee alumni contributions also reflect this emphasis. The analysis did, in fact, find that corporations engaged in labor-intensive production gave proportionately more than those engaged in capital-intensive production.

This finding has relevance in evaluating the growth in corporate giving propensities discovered in the time-series analysis. As corporate activity has become more capital intensive, the pressure to give arising from employee-related programs presumably has declined in relative importance. If this is the case, the growth in giving propensity was even greater than that measured by the time-series analysis. Unfortunately it was not possible explicitly to include the trend toward capital-intensive production in the time-series analysis.

Company-Sponsored Foundations

Beginning with World War II, and principally since 1950, corporations have made widespread use of company-sponsored foundations in their giving programs. It was estimated that, in the 1956–1965 decade, about one-fourth of total corporate contributions were channeled through company-sponsored foundations. Such foundations usually serve only as conduits for corporate giving and as reservoirs to permit the stabilization of payments to philanthropic recipients. Some foundations, however, have accumulated substantial endowments well in excess of those needed to stabilize income-outlay flows. Where this has occurred, there is an initial lag in the corporation's contributions to charity, as a large part of contributions are used to build endowment. This is followed by an increased flow of funds to charity, as investment earnings on endowment augment the corporation's contributions.

Most of the endowment growth of company-sponsored foundations took place in the early 1950's, years when the Korean War excess-profits tax provided a strong incentive to contributions. It is estimated that the endowment of all company-sponsored foundations increased by about $400 million in that period. Since then the growth has been much slower, but considerable, nonetheless. In 1956–1960 it is estimated to have grown by $65 million, and from 1961 to 1964 by $90 million.

The effect of endowment building on the over-all flow of contributions to philanthropic agencies generally has been small. In the period from 1956 through 1964, despite an estimated $155 million applied to increase foundation endowments, philanthropic agencies received about 3 per cent more than corporations gave in the period. The difference, of course, reflects investment earnings applied to philanthropic programs. Probably only in the early 1950's did endowment building have a significant effect. The estimated $400 million applied to increase endowments in that period meant that philanthropic agencies received about 11 per cent less than corporations gave. Barring a return to extremely high tax rates, it seems unlikely that such a pattern would appear again.

TWO

〒〒〒

The Focus
and Growth
of Corporation
Giving

CORPORATION GIVING accounts for a relatively small share of total private giving. In 1962 it amounted to a little less than one-twentieth of the total (*Table 3*). Part of the reason for this is that about three-fifths of total contributions are to religious institutions, and this represents the contributions of individuals and families almost exclusively.

If one excludes gifts to religious institutions, the share of corporations is doubled to about 9 per cent (*Table 4*). There is some justification for excluding religion from the total. Though voluntary in the United States, most of religious giving may be regarded as the price of membership in an organization, one, to be sure, which provides a significant part of the ethical and philosophical underpinnings of philanthropy. Contributions are principally used to support the local church and church school, with only a small fraction directed into traditional philanthropic and welfare activities.

Though corporation giving accounts for only 9 per cent of total nonreligious giving, in a number of fields its share is much larger. One dollar in every seven given to higher education is given by corporations, while one in every three dollars of support for community chests and united funds is a corporate dollar (*Table 4*).

Though small in relation to total private giving, corporate giving may have had a disproportionate impact, at least in certain areas. With the possible exception of foundation giving, corporation giving

13

TABLE 3   Estimated Total Gifts and Contributions by Major Classes of Donor, 1962 (Dollar values in millions)

	Amount	Percentage of Total
1. Gifts of living donors	$9,980	78.2
2. Foundation expenditures on philanthropic program	1,012	7.9
3. Charitable bequests	876	6.9
4. Corporation gifts and contributions	595	4.7
5. Endowment income of colleges, universities, and hospitals	300	2.4

SOURCES: *Row 1:* U.S. Internal Revenue Service, *Statistics of Income, Individual Tax Returns for 1962* (Washington, 1961), Table E, p. 6. Itemized deductions totaling $7,516,000 were increased by estimates of contributions of persons and families using the standard deduction or not required to file a return. *Row 2:* Committee on Ways and Means, U.S. House of Representatives, *Treasury Department Report on Private Foundations,* February 2, 1965, Table 10, p. 79. *Row 3:* U.S. Internal Revenue Service *Statistics of Income, 1962, Fiduciary, Gift, and Estate Tax Returns* (Washington, 1965), Table 1, p. 62. *Row 4:* U.S. Internal Revenue Service, *Statistics of Income, 1962, Corporation Income Tax Returns* (Washington, 1966), Table 2, p. 58. *Row 5: The 1962 Study of College and University Endowment Funds* (Boston: The Boston Fund, 1963), extrapolated.

TABLE 4   Estimated Corporation Support[a] of Selected Types of Philanthropic Organizations, 1962

	Percentage of Total Corporate Giving	Corporate Support as Percentage of Total Philanthropic Support
Churches and church schools	0.6	0.03
Philanthropic institutions other than churches and church schools	99.4	9.0
Higher education	34.0	14.0
Federated community health and welfare	29.0	34.0
Other welfare, health, and hospital	17.0	n.d.[b]
Independent private secondary schools	0.2	3.0

[a] Includes contributions channeled through company-sponsored foundations.
[b] No data available.

has probably undergone a more pronounced change of emphasis than other sources of private philanthropy. It may have made the difference between success and failure in individual undertakings, particularly in the relatively new field of support for cultural projects.

THE GROWTH OF CORPORATION GIVING
RELATIVE TO OTHER COMPONENTS OF PRIVATE PHILANTHROPY

Despite their small share in total private philanthropy, corporation contributions probably have grown more rapidly than those of any

TABLE 5   Estimated Philanthropic Contributions by Living Donors, Bequests,
and Corporations, 1936–1939, 1960 and 1962
(Dollar values in millions)

Period	Living Donors (Individuals and Families)	Charitable Bequests	Corpo- rations
Average, 1936–39	$1,055	$159	$ 30
Average, 1960 and 1962	9,584	913	539
1960 and 1962 average as percentage of 1936–39 average	910%	570%	1800%

SOURCE: U.S. Internal Revenue Service, *Statistics of Income* for: *Individual Income Tax Returns* (extrapolated); *Fiduciary, Gift, and Estate Tax Returns;* and *Corporation Income Tax Returns.*

other type of donors. Historical data are not available for all classes of donors, but it is possible to compare the growth of corporate giving with two of the three largest kinds of donors (*Table 5*). As the table shows, estimated giving by corporations in 1960 and 1962 was much higher relative to its 1936–1939 level than giving by either families and individuals or by charitable bequest. No comprehensive estimate exists on giving in the late 1930's by philanthropic foundations, the third of the largest kinds of donors; however, $70 million might not be too far from the mark.[1] If so, then the ratio of the 1960 and 1962 average to that of 1936–1939 would be on the order of 12 to 14, or between that of individual and family giving on the one hand, and corporate giving on the other.

HISTORICAL DEVELOPMENT OF GIVING

The history of modern corporate giving begins in the 1870's and reflects the elaboration of the business corporation and its growth to

---

[1] For further detail on this estimate, see Ralph L. Nelson, *The Investment Policies of Foundations* (New York: Russell Sage Foundation, 1967), p. 3. Another estimate has placed foundation expenditures, predominantly grants, at $72 million in 1944: F. Emerson Andrews, *Philanthropic Foundations* (New York: Russell Sage Foundation, 1956), Table 3, p. 17. In the early 1960's, probably between 15 and 20 per cent of foundation spending was that of company-sponsored foundations. As most of this represented current or near-current gifts from corporations, there is some double counting in Table 1, and an overstatement in the size of giving by foundations not affiliated with corporations. As company-sponsored foundations were relatively insignificant in the late 1930's, there is also some overstatement in the estimate of growth in noncorporate foundation giving. Because the adjustment would not be large enough to affect comparative magnitudes, and because precise estimates are lacking, no attempt was made to adjust the data for such double counting.

preëminence in the organization and conduct of economic activity.[2] In the last quarter of the nineteenth century, practically all corporate giving was by railroad companies in support of Young Men's Christian Associations. It was probably not difficult to convince shareholders of the value to the company of these contributions for, among other things, the "Y"s provided economical accommodations for train crews laying over at the end of their runs. Indeed, many were established and supported by railroad companies for this very purpose. After 1900 the YMCA was successful in enlisting support from other kinds of industrial corporations.

The acceleration and diversification of corporate giving had to await the United States' entry into World War I. At that time, the YMCA and the Red Cross, which were enlisted to raise funds through national wartime campaigns, were apparently quite successful in obtaining corporate contributions. Precise data are not available, but it is probable that corporations donated between $40 and $50 million to the wartime drives of the Red Cross and YMCA in 1917 and a substantially higher amount in 1918. In his review of this period, F. Emerson Andrews concluded: "Certainly enough evidence exists to pin-point 1917 as the year in which corporation contributions first reached a substantial total in the history of American philanthropy."[3]

Corporation giving dropped sharply after World War I, and apparently did not return to its World War I levels until World War II. An earlier study of the National Bureau of Economic Research revealed that, in 1920, corporate contributions to community chests totaled between $2.5 and $3 million.[4] Although this total grew fivefold through the 1920's, in the main this was found to reflect the spread of the community chest movement in this decade, rather than a major increase in corporation giving. For the thirteen community chests submitting data for 1920, corporate contributions declined in 1921 and 1922 and, after seven successive yearly increases, were 10 per cent higher in 1929 than in 1920. The corporations' share in the total support of the thirteen chests declined slightly, from 24 per cent in 1920 to 23 per cent in 1929. It seems likely that the spread of the

---

[2] This brief historical summary is drawn principally from F. Emerson Andrews, *Corporation Giving* (New York: Russell Sage Foundation, 1952), Chapter 2, and from Pierce Williams and Frederick E. Croxton, *Corporation Contributions to Organized Community Welfare Services* (New York: National Bureau of Economic Research, 1930), particularly for the period 1910–1929.

[3] Andrews, *Corporation Giving*, p. 28.

[4] Williams and Croxton, *op. cit.*, p. 11.

community chest movement was more of a spur to corporate giving in this decade than the other way around.

Precise estimates for the period 1930–1935 are not available.[5] In broad outline, the pattern seems consistent with Andrews' findings that, despite reduced sales and profits, many corporations actively responded to the emergency drives of the early Depression years and often their 1935 contributions were above those for 1929.[6] However, given the economic stringencies of the period, it is not likely that over-all rates could have been sustained or increased.

Comprehensive direct data on corporation giving begin in 1936, the first year in which contributions were made deductible from income in determining income tax liability. Tabulations based on corporate income tax returns indicate that, from 1936 through 1939, annual contributions followed a flat pattern, totaling successively $30, $33, $27, and $31 million.

The onset of World War II led to sharp increases in corporation giving. By 1942, the first full year of total United States involvement in the war, contributions had reached almost $100 million. One year later they were $159 million. The next year, 1944, they grew to $234 million, and by 1945, had reached $266 million, or almost nine times their 1939 level. In this six-year period, corporate philanthropy not only grew significantly, but set the stage for continued growth, albeit at a less spectacular rate. In the four years 1946–1949, corporate contributions averaged $229 million; in 1950–1954, $361 million; in 1955–1959, $425 million; and in 1960–1964, $595 million.

To summarize, in the quarter-century from the late 1930's to the early 1960's, corporate giving increased from an annual rate of $31

---

[5] One series exists, but no claims are made for its usefulness in making year-to-year comparisons:

Year	Amount in Millions
1929	$22
1930	35
1931	40
1932	31
1933	27
1934	27
1935	28

These figures are from the U.S. Department of Commerce, *U.S. Income and Output, A Supplement to the Survey of Current Business* (Washington, 1958), Table 1–12, pp. 134–135. Estimates of corporate giving were made in the interests of comparable and comprehensive national income and product accounts for the period before direct tax return data became available. Although considered adequate for this purpose, and of the right order of magnitude, no claim is made for their detailed accuracy.

[6] Andrews, *Corporation Giving*, pp. 35–37.

million to one of $595 million—nineteenfold. It is this period that is
the principal concern of this study.

RELATION OF GIVING TO THE GROSS NATIONAL PRODUCT

In the first five years of the 1960's, corporation gifts and contributions reported on tax returns averaged $595 million a year. In the
same period, the gross national product averaged $560 billion. Thus,
corporate contributions supported the production of slightly more
than one-tenth of 1 per cent of total national economic product. One
dollar of every thousand spent by all purchasers of goods and services
was spent by corporations when, through the medium of philanthropic contributions, they "purchased" the welfare, health, educational, and other services rendered to the public by philanthropic
organizations.

In dollar value the level of corporation giving in the early 1960's
was the highest it has been. It passed the $500-million mark for the
first time in 1961 and rose to $729 million in 1964. However, relative
to the gross national product, it has held quite constant since the middle of World War II (*Chart A*). In the four war years, 1942–1945,
contributions averaged $189 million a year, or almost one-tenth of 1
per cent of the average gross national product of $193 billion for
those four years. Since then, except for a few departures associated
with the imposition and repeal of the excess-profits tax, the share
held close to one-tenth of 1 per cent in each year.

The United States' entry into World War II was the occasion of a
great expansion in corporate giving. In the last four years of the
1930's, corporate giving averaged $30 million per year; in the four
war years, as just mentioned, it averaged $189 million. It was in this
period that giving's share of the national product increased sharply,
from one-thirtieth to one-tenth of 1 per cent of the gross national
product.

The growth in dollar values of corporate giving and gross national
product overstates the growth in the amount of economic activity
represented by these measures. From the late 1930's to the early
1960's the level of prices increased about two-and-one-half times. For
a comparison based on dollars of 1936 value, the observed values for
the early 1960's, therefore, must be reduced to about two-fifths of
their current dollar values. However, even when the dollar series are
so deflated, the growth in corporation giving is considerable. In dollars of constant (1936) value, corporate giving rose from a 1936–1939
average of $29.6 million to a 1942–1945 average of $140.1 million, or

CHART A   Corporation Giving Relative to Gross National Product, 1936–1964

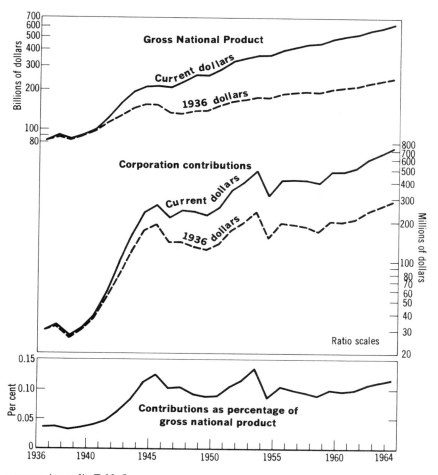

SOURCE: Appendix Table I.

by 4.7 times—an annual compound interest rate of 29.6 per cent. It further increased from its 1942–1945 average of $140.1 million to an average of $239.3 million in 1960–1964, again in dollars of 1936 value. The 1942–1945 to 1960–1964 increase of 71 per cent was at an annual compound interest rate of 2.9 per cent for the period.

The adjustment for price-level changes does not affect the analysis of the share of gross national product accounted for by corporation giving, since the same price index was used to deflate contributions and gross national product. For the purpose of making a rough adjustment for the large increase in price levels over the period, this procedure was sufficient. No effort was made to identify differential price-level changes between corporation giving and the economy in general. No index of the "market basket" of services purchased by corporate contributions exists, nor is it clear just how one might go about developing one. A review of existing price indexes for more specific parts of the economy (e.g., the consumer price index) did not suggest that any single one might be more appropriate than the implicit price deflator for the gross national product.

RELATION OF GIVING TO CORPORATE NET INCOME

The rapid increase in corporation giving relative to national product in the period from 1936 to World War II, and the maintenance of the share of giving in national product since then, invites an examination of some of the developments that accompanied this pattern of growth. The period was marked by significant changes in the earnings and tax treatment of business corporations. The number of active corporations grew by one-and-one-half times over the period, while the number reporting net taxable income grew by two-and-one-half times. The percentage of corporation income captured in income and excess-profits taxes ranged from 13 to 56 per cent of before-tax income, and the period included two peaks of tax liability, both associated with a wartime economy. The device of the company-sponsored foundation came to play a significant role in the flow of corporate contributions, and major changes took place in the direction of giving, and in the kinds of recipients receiving contributions.

The development having the most direct bearing on corporation giving is the growth in corporate income or profit, and this will be examined first. For a number of legal reasons, corporate income is the only resource from which the company may make contributions. Unlike personal giving, which may involve the distribution of accumulated personal wealth, corporations are more restricted in the distribution of their wealth. The prior claims of creditors and owners are explicitly recognized and safeguarded, and careful distinctions are made between the distribution of capital as against income. Moreover, the net-income base for corporate giving has specific recognition in the Internal Revenue Code provision that corporations may not deduct as contributions more than 5 per cent of income in arriving at taxable income.

In comparing the trends of corporate profit and giving, the record for corporations reporting a taxable income will be examined separately from those reporting no net income. The giving performance of the latter group can be expected to be much lower than that of the group reporting profits. Not only is giving likely to be curtailed or abandoned when there are zero profits, or losses, but the tax incentive to give is also absent. Since deductions for contributions are limited to 5 per cent of income, when there is zero or negative income the allowable deduction falls to zero.[7]

Examination of the historical record confirms the prediction that the difference in giving levels between the two groups is marked. In the period from 1940 through 1964, contributions of corporations without net income never exceeded 3 per cent of total reported contributions. In nineteen of these twenty-five years, they were less than 1.5 per cent of the total. Nor was this low percentage merely indicative of the fact that corporations reporting no net income accounted for an equally low percentage of total corporate activity. Their share of total expenditures for all purposes, as reported on tax returns, ranged from 4 to 18 per cent, and in thirteen of the twenty-four years it exceeded 10 per cent. The "no-net-income" corporations' yearly share of total corporate activity, thus measured, averaged about 9.3 times their share of total contributions for the same year.

If the 1.4 per cent of contributions reported by corporations with no net income were included in the analysis of the trend in giving rates, their negative net income would also have to be included. As shown below, in Chart C, the inclusion of this negative income would reduce the income base by a sharply fluctuating percentage, ranging from 4 to 40 per cent. If total corporation net income were used as the base, the time pattern would reflect, in uneven fashion, the differential giving rates of corporations with and without net income. The inclusion of corporations with no net income might serve more to complicate the analysis of the trend than to simplify it.

Contributions by Corporations with
  Profits

The most meaningful measure of income for our purposes was considered to be corporation net income after taxes and before gifts and contributions. Because corporate contributions, averaging three-quarters of 1 per cent of before-tax income, were one of the smallest and most discretionary items of outlay, it was felt that they could

---

[7] This rule was modified in 1953 to allow a two-year carry-forward of contributions in excess of 5 per cent of income in a particular year. The effect of this modification is examined in a later section of this chapter.

have had little if any effect on the time pattern of the divergence between before- and after-tax income. After-tax income, in this context, reflected the less ambiguous measure of corporate ability to pay and was, therefore, taken as the basis for comparison.

The income measure was further refined by putting it on a "before contributions" basis. This was done by adding to corporation income after taxes and after all deductions the net after-tax cost of contributions. This produced an estimate of the after-tax income that corporations must have earned to obtain the net income they reported after they had made their contributions and taken their allowed deduction. The net after-tax cost was calculated by multiplying the reported contributions by the complement of the estimated marginal tax rate. While this refinement was desirable for conceptual purity, its effect on the observed trend in after-tax income and on that in giving rates is insignificant.

It is clear that corporate giving received its greatest impetus in periods of war (*Chart B*). The trend in dollar value of gifts and contributions, again adjusted for price-level changes, is marked by two periods of sharply increased giving levels: 1943 to 1945, the major years of World War II, and 1951 to 1953, the Korean War years. However, the endings of these periods of national mobilization were not marked by a return to prewar levels. Indeed, in dollars of comparable value, giving in 1962–1964 averaged 30 per cent higher than in the three peak Korean War Years and 64 per cent higher than in the three peak World War II years.

The sustained increase in giving is more clearly evident when compared with corporate after-tax income. The rate rose sharply during both World War II and the Korean War and declined sharply at the end of the two wartime periods. In neither case, however, did the decline involve a return to prewar giving rates. In 1936–1939, contributions averaged 0.35 per cent of corporate after-tax income; in 1946–1949, this had risen to 1.03 per cent; in 1955–1959, to 1.41 per cent; and in 1960–1964, to 1.58 per cent. Excluding the war years, then, the increase is a fairly linear one, with the percentage of income increasing by one-twentieth of one percentage point a year.

Contributions by Corporations
  Having Losses
An interesting, if minor, part of corporate philanthropy is giving by corporations having zero or negative net income. As was shown above, such corporations give proportionately less, relative to the size

CHART B   Corporation Giving Relative to Net Income, Corporations with Net Income, Constant (1936) Dollars, 1936–1964

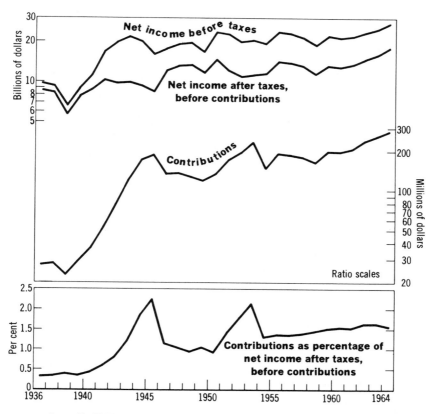

of their activities, than do companies having profits, and this is probably to be expected. For corporations in strained financial condition, the need to make ordinary business outlays must certainly take priority over giving, and their tax incentive is blunted as well. Nonetheless, over the twenty-nine-year period of 1936 through 1964, corporations with zero or negative net income made contributions aggregating $118 million, 1.4 per cent of total corporate contributions for the period.

In the late 1930's, giving by loss corporations averaged about 11 per cent of all corporate giving. This was a much higher proportion than in any year since then. Corporate earnings in 1936–1939 were generally low, and reflected the economic depression of that decade. A large part of corporation activity was conducted by companies not yet on a profitable basis. In these four years, total expenditures by no-net-income corporations ranged from 23 to 37 per cent of expenditures by all corporations. In no year since then has the percentage been more than 18 per cent. Though loss corporations did not give as much in proportion to total outlays as did those with profits, their greater importance in this four-year period boosted their over-all share of corporate giving.[8] In addition, contributions from profitable corporations were also low in these depression years, so that the modest contributions from loss corporations made up a higher fraction of the total.[9] Tax deductibility, introduced in 1936, plus the relatively low tax rates of the time were apparently not sufficient to offer more than a modest inducement to corporate giving.

Giving by loss corporations continued at low levels until 1954. Thereafter the absolute amount rose significantly, and the higher level has been sustained. Their share of total corporate contributions also rose somewhat. Part of the explanation for this upward movement may be the increase in the proportion of corporate activity accounted for by loss corporations, an increase which has been quite persistent since World War II (*Chart C*). Probably more pertinent is the enactment, effective in 1954, of a two-year carry-forward of the deduction for contributions in excess of the maximum of 5 per cent of income allowed for any given year.[10] Corporations with losses in a given year, if anticipating profits in the following years, would be more willing to make current contributions than they would have been in the absence of this provision.

THE NUMBER OF COMPANIES MAKING CONTRIBUTIONS

One factor which may have contributed to the increase in the share of corporate income given to philanthropy is the adoption of giving policies by an increasing proportion of corporations. Although there is no direct evidence of such a trend, rising corporate incomes and

---

[8] The number and deficit of loss corporations relative to the number and income of profitable corporations may be overstated for the first six years relative to the remainder of the period. From 1936 through 1941, the privilege of filing consolidated income tax returns was restricted to railroads and Pan American Trade Corporations. In 1942 it was made more generally available, so that some subsidiary corporations with losses, previously filing unconsolidated returns, would no longer appear among the loss corporations. The numbers, income or loss, and contributions reported on consolidated returns were small, however, and so the effect of the change on the observed time pattern is likely to be minimal.

[9] Contributions of profit corporations averaged only 0.35 per cent of average after-tax income of $7.7 billion.

[10] Section 170 (b) (2), 1954 Internal Revenue Code.

CHART C   Numbers, Deficits, and Contributions of Corporations with Zero or Negative Income, 1936–1964

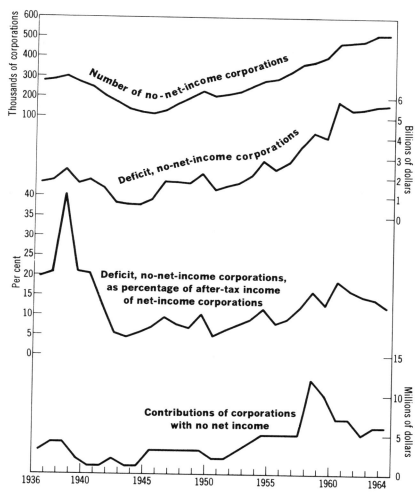

SOURCE: Appendix Table IV.

income tax rates, together with the newly legislated deductibility of gifts, must have made increasing numbers of companies aware of the advantages of giving. This, combined with war-expanded appeals from welfare organizations, the Red Cross, and other servicemen's aid groups, appears likely to have led an increasing percentage of companies to initiate giving programs which, once the war was over, were probably maintained, though perhaps at a lower level.

TABLE 6   Percentage of Corporations Reporting Contributions and Reporting Net Income, by Asset Size, 1958

Asset-Size Class (Thousands)	Contributions (Millions) (1)	Number of Corporations (2)	Percentage Reporting Contri- butions (3)	Net Income (4)
TOTAL	$395.4	990,381	27.7	61.7
Zero assets or assets not reported	3.0	62,746	9.4	38.9
Under $100	7.8	537,338	17.9	54.6
$100, under $1,000	58.1	329,682	40.9	74.6
$1,000, under $10,000	92.0	51,191	60.4	79.0
$10,000, under $100,000	93.4	8,221	63.2	75.8
$100,000 and over	141.1	1,203	66.6	87.0

SOURCE: *Columns 1, 2, and 4:* U.S. Internal Revenue Service *Statistics of Income 1958–59, Corporation Income Tax Returns,* pp. 39–40, 145–46; *Column 3:* U.S. Internal Revenue Service, *Statistics of Income, 1959–1960, Corporation Income Tax Returns Addendum: Statistics of Income 1958–59,* Frequency of Returns for Balance Sheet and Income Statement Items, pp. 243–254.

Unfortunately the absence of data does not permit a documentation of this surmise. The only direct data on numbers of corporations reporting contributions are for the year 1958, the result of a special tabulation by the Internal Revenue Service of the numbers of corporations reporting specific balance sheet and income statement items on corporate income tax returns.[11] In interpreting these data the characteristics of the year 1958 require particular attention.

For 1958, 990,381 active corporations filed income tax returns. Of these, 273,909, or 27.7 per cent, reported contributions or gifts. In the aggregate, therefore, only about one in four corporations appears to have made contributions. Lest the mistaken impression be given that total contributions would increase by a factor of 3 or 4 were all corporations to adopt a policy of giving, the following patterns should be kept in mind.

First, the proportion of large corporations that reported contributions is much higher than that for small corporations (*Table 6*). This may be because small corporations are more likely to regard local contributions as expenses and not report them as "contributions." Corporations having $1 million or more in assets, while representing

---

[11] U.S. Internal Revenue Service, *Statistics of Income, 1959–1960, Corporation Income Tax Returns Addendum: Statistics of Income 1958–59,* Frequency of Returns for Balance Sheet and Income Statement Items, pp. 243–254.

only 6.1 per cent of the number of active corporations, accounted for 82.6 per cent of total contributions.

Second, a large percentage of corporations report zero or negative net income. In 1958 this percentage was 38.3, that is, about two out of five corporations had little immediate financial encouragement or tax inducement to make contributions. The data do not show how many profit and how many loss corporations reported contributions, nor was it clear how one should go about making a plausible division of the total. Were separate data available, it would seem reasonable to expect to find a much smaller percentage of loss than of profit corporations reporting contributions. Over the ten years from 1954 to 1964, the proportion of loss corporations ranged between 36 and 41 per cent. It follows that a large minority of active corporations in any given year is not in a financial position favorable to the making of gifts even though, as a general policy, it makes contributions when circumstances permit.

Third, 1958 was a year of economic recession, reduced corporate profits, and low total contributions (*Chart D*). For these reasons, the percentage of companies electing to distribute a part of income to philanthropy was probably lower than normal. If so, then this, too, leads to an understatement in the percentage of companies that pursue a general policy of contributing to philanthropy.

One other factor may have had an influence on the statistics: the company-sponsored foundations, which have been established by a number of corporations to serve as conduits for their philanthropic contributions. Corporations frequently make grants to their foundations once in every two or three years, with the intention that the foundations will spread their disbursements to philanthropy over several years. The reservoir is usually replenished in years of high profits when corporations are best able to so distribute their income. Since 1958 was a year of low profits, such reservoir-building grants may well have been deferred. If the foundations continued to spend from their balances, the flow of contributions to recipients would be relatively unaffected, even though corporations would report no contributions on their tax returns.

When the several factors described above are taken into consideration, the impression remains that the practice of corporation giving is much more widespread than indicated by the gross percentage of corporations reporting contributions. Certainly, considerable room exists for increasing the number of corporations that follow a policy

CHART D   Patterns of Corporate Giving and Income in the Recession
Year 1958

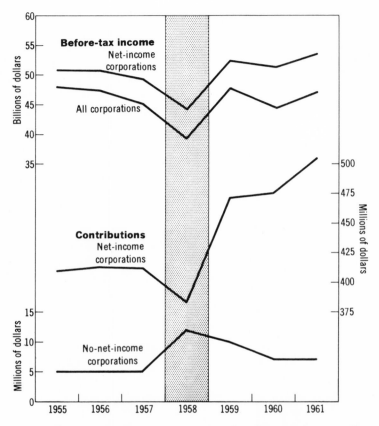

NOTE: Shaded area represents year for which data on number of corporations reporting
contributions were given.
SOURCE: Appendix Tables III and IV.

of giving. However, in terms of the potential dollar addition to total
corporate giving that would result from more widespread giving, the
prospect is a much more modest one.

TRENDS IN NET AFTER-TAX OUTLAYS FOR CONTRIBUTIONS

In addition to widening the difference between the before-tax and
after-tax income of corporations, the rise in tax rates has reduced the
net after-tax cost of a given amount of contributions. This, of course,
results from the fact that contributions are deductible from income

CHART E   Net After-Tax Cost of Contributions Relative to After-Tax Income Corporations with Net Income, 1936–64

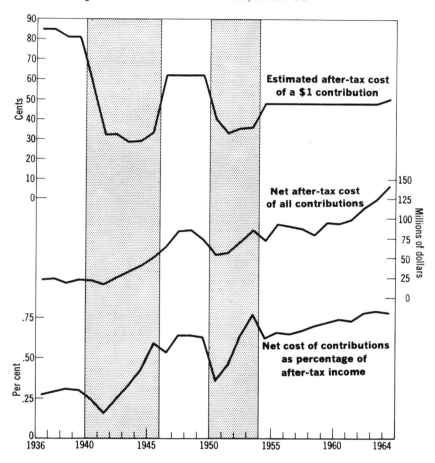

NOTE: Shaded areas represent excess-profits tax years.
SOURCE: Appendix Tables II, V, and VI.

in computing a corporation's taxable income. The decline in after-tax cost is described in the top panel of Chart E, and the method of computing the net after-tax cost is given in Chapter Three, where an analysis of its effect on contributions is made.

Not all of the observed rise in giving represents an increase in the net burden of gifts and contributions to corporations. The rise in corporate income tax rates and the deductibility of contributions in computing taxable income indicate that an increasing percentage of corporation giving has been supported by the general public as represented by the tax collector.

Despite the increase in tax rates, the net after-tax outlay for contributions grew significantly over the period. As shown in the middle panel of Chart E, it grew from an annual average of $22 million dollars in 1935–1939 to $115 million in 1960–1964, in dollars of comparable (1936) purchasing power. For corporations with net income, the real net burden of contributions thus increased more than fivefold over the period.

The period, of course, also saw a significant rise in the ability of corporations to make contributions. In 1936 dollars, corporate income after taxes rose from a 1936–1939 average of $7,605 million to a 1960–1964 average of $14,946 million. However, this was less than a twofold increase, compared with a fivefold increase in their net after-tax outlays for contributions. Therefore, as shown in the bottom-panel of Chart E, the increase in the net cost of contributions as a percentage of after-tax income almost tripled.

These data clearly reveal that, over this twenty-eight-year period, the net burden of corporate philanthropy relative to corporate disposable income has increased substantially, though still accounting for less than 1 per cent of corporate disposable income. Most noteworthy, perhaps, is the almost unbroken rise since 1954, through a period when no change in tax rates altered the "price" inducement to make contributions.

INTERPRETATION OF TAX RETURN DATA

The trends described above are based on data taken from the income tax returns of corporations. As such, they reflect those categories of corporate expenditures that the Internal Revenue Service accepts as being philanthropic in character. They also reflect the heterogeneous collection of industrial, commercial, professional, and, in part, personal endeavors that have adopted the corporate form of organization.

The trend described by these data may depart in some degree from one based on purely "corporate" and purely "philanthropic" concepts of corporate giving, but there was no feasible way of obtaining these more refined measures. However, some indications of the importance of such "impurities" in the tax return data are presented so that an evaluation of the observed trends might be made.

Philanthropic Outlays Included as
Business Expense

Some of the contributions that corporations make to organizations in the health, welfare, or educational fields are deducted, not as philanthropic contributions, but as business expenses. If treated in this manner, they escape the 5 per cent limitation. This is probably not a significant factor, however, since so few companies give enough to approach this percentage of income. Most often, the contribution is judged to be closely related to the corporation's activities, providing a fairly direct benefit to the company. An example would be a paint company's grant to support research in colloidal chemistry at a local university, as the results may prove to be of fairly direct benefit to the company. In one sense, the grant is a philanthropic contribution to an educational institution. In another—and probably equally accurate— sense it is payment for off-premises research that might have been as readily contracted with a commercial research company.[12]

The Internal Revenue data do not provide any basis for estimating the outlays that fall near the fuzzy boundary between business expense and philanthropic contribution. Some direct evidence was developed by the Russell Sage Foundation in a 1950 survey of the giving policies of 326 corporations. Data developed by the survey suggest that reported contributions would be increased by about 8 per cent, if payments for health, welfare, educational or religious purposes that were actually taken as business expenses had been counted as philanthropic contributions instead (*Table 7*).

Because the survey covers only one year, it provides no way of determining whether such "hidden contributions" have represented an increasing or declining share of total corporate giving.[13] One might speculate that this share was high in 1936 and for several years after. As no provision for tax deductibility existed before 1936,

---

[12] Some have suggested that the definition of a company contribution should turn on the intent of the donor. Although this definition was appealing on principle, no attempt was made to recast the data on this basis, since the problems of definition and classification were held much too complex to permit defensible estimates.

[13] Professor Willard Thorp has suggested that the growth in reported contributions might be lower to the degree that corporations have provided their own medical staffs and facilities, than if they had continued to support community-wide general purpose medical facilities. Unfortunately, no data are available to measure the importance of this shift. Another reviewer, on the other hand, cited the practice of corporations, when making contributions to local hospitals, of asking the hospital to set aside space for emergency use of its employees.

TABLE 7   Contributions Treated as Charitable Deductions and Business
Expenses, 326 Surveyed Corporations, 1950 (Dollar values in thousands)

| | Gifts Reported as | | |
| | Contributions (1) | Business Expense (2) | (2) as Percentage of (1) |
Asset Size			
Under $1 million	$ 91	$ 13	14.9
$1 to $50 million	1,544	190	12.3
$50 million and over	4,675	276	5.9
TOTAL	$6,310	$479	7.6

SOURCE: Based on F. Emerson Andrews, *Corporation Giving* (New York: Russell Sage Foundation, 1952), Table 40, p. 252.

earlier outlays having a strong element of philanthropy were probably included in some plausible category of business expense. In the period of adjustment following the tax-deductibility provision this practice may have continued for a while. However, with the rapid increase of giving during World War II, a new balance may have rapidly evolved. The pattern observed for 1950, therefore, may have been fairly characteristic of the whole period since World War II, which has seen sustained high levels of both contributions and tax rates.

The Mixture of Family and Corporate
Giving in the Small Corporation

One important way in which corporations differ is in the degree to which personal or family interests enter their policies. At the one extreme are the very large corporations, the ownership of which is widely dispersed and which are operated by salaried professional managers. At the other extreme are the small, owner-managed businesses that, for one reason or another, have chosen to adopt the corporate form in preference to proprietorship or partnership. In the large corporation, the giving decision is more likely to be made in terms of broad, nonpersonal objectives; the corporation is viewed as an institution having an existence independent of the individuals associated with it. In the small corporation, the objectives of the owners and the business are more thoroughly intermingled, and the giving decisions are more likely to reflect the personal preferences of the owner-manager.

The channeling of what is essentially personal giving through corporations has probably been encouraged by the provisions of the tax laws. The tax-saving possibilities of the corporate contributions deduction have been summarized in the following succinct fashion:

> John Brown, who owns or controls all the stock in the John Brown Company, has been asked to contribute to a building fund for Alma Mater College. Recent profits having been good, he decides to give $1,000. He can—
>
> *a.* Vote himself an additional $1,000 in dividends and pay by personal check. His contribution credit on personal income is now exactly balanced by his added income, so there is no saving here. Meanwhile, the John Brown Company had to make $2,083 so that Mr. Brown could take out $1,000 net profit, after the 52 per cent tax.
>
> *b.* Set aside the same $2,083. Pay $1,000 by company check. Pay the 52 per cent tax on the remaining $1,083 and pocket the balance of about $520 as profit for his sagacity.
>
> *c.* Set aside the same $2,083, and pay the whole amount to the College by company check. He more than doubles the contribution at the same cost as a $1,000 personal contribution.
>
> Company contributions in discharge of personal obligations may be part of the explanation for the notably higher contribution rate of the smaller companies. One chain store reports that its contribution budget has to be unusually large to meet "the heavy competition in contributions from local merchants who are able to make personal gifts through their stores and thereby deduct the corporation tax."[14]

Internal Revenue Service data do not classify corporations by their patterns of ownership, and so differences in giving rates and patterns between publicly held and owner-managed corporations cannot be measured. However, some limited evidence on such differences is provided by data gathered in a National Industrial Conference Board survey for 1962 (*Table 8*). The twelve largest corporate givers in the survey, each with total contributions of at least $2 million, presumably represented large, widely held corporations. From them, education received 48 per cent of the contributions dollar, and health and welfare, 35 per cent. The twelve smallest corporate givers in the survey, each with total contributions of no more than $1,900, presumably were more representative of the small family corporation. From them, health and welfare received 72 per cent of the contributions dollar, and education, only 12 per cent.

A special 1962 tabulation of contributions reported on individual income tax returns makes it possible to identify which of the two patterns of corporate contributions more closely approximates that of

---

[14] Andrews, *Corporation Giving*, pp. 248–249.

TABLE 8   The Composition of Contributions: Large Corporations, Small Corporations, and Individuals, 1962

	Percentage of Contributions		
Recipient	*12 Largest Company Budgets*	*12 Smallest Company Budgets*	*Itemized on Individual Income Tax Returns*
Health and welfare	35.3	72.4	15.7
(federated drives)	(21.5)	(50.7)	(*n.a.*)
Education	47.8	11.8	3.6
(secondary education)	(3.1)	(0.0)	(*n.a.*)
Religious organizations	0.04	0.9	60.9
Civic and cultural	3.7	5.5 ⎫	19.8
Other	13.1	9.4 ⎬	
	100.0	100.0	100.0
Average budget size	$5,663,000	$1,203	—

Contributions to Health-Welfare and Education Only

Health and welfare	42.5	86.0	81.1
Education	57.5	14.0	18.9
	100.0	100.0	100.0

NOTE: Detail may not add to totals because of rounding.
SOURCES: *Companies:* The National Industrial Conference Board, *Business Management Record,* October, 1963, pp. 31–32; *Individuals:* U.S. Treasury Department *Statistics of Income: Individual Income Tax Returns for 1962,* p. 6.

personal giving. As Table 8 shows, the pattern of personal giving departs from that of corporate giving in one important respect: the prominence of giving to religious organizations, which is virtually absent, not only in the large, but also in small corporations. The legal and philosophical deterrents to the support of religion by the large corporate givers with widespread ownership are well known. That small givers show a similar pattern may indicate a feeling that support of religion is more properly the responsibility of the individual and, tax advantages notwithstanding, is not to be channeled through the family corporation.

A more meaningful comparison, therefore, is provided by excluding the religious organizations from the data on personal giving.[15] This is

---

[15] The "Other" category is also excluded from the comparison, because its content is not well enough known and possibly differs widely as between corporations and individuals. It is probable that a significant part of the 20 per cent of personal contributions in the "Other" category represent transfers to family foundations, the ultimate recipients of which are not specified. On the other hand, the corporate contributions breakdown includes the outlays of company-sponsored foundations, and so the "Other" category represents activities not otherwise listed in the table.

done in the bottom panel of Table 8, which compares the balance between gifts to health and welfare in one row and to education in the other. As one might expect, the pattern for the small corporate givers is much closer to that for individuals than is the pattern for the large corporations.

The tax inducements to personal giving through family-controlled corporations have probably meant that an increasing percentage of what appears in the Internal Revenue Service statistics as corporate giving represents merely a shift from personal giving rather than a net increase in total giving. However, it is doubtful that this shift would contribute significantly to the observed, strongly upward trend in corporate giving. This is because the preponderance of corporation giving is done by the largest corporations, where family control is less common. In 1962, for example, the 5,222 largest corporations, each with assets of $25 million or more, made contributions totaling $366 million, or 62 per cent of the contributions made by all corporations.

THREE
⟁⟁⟁

Economic
Analysis
of Corporate
Giving

THE RAPID growth of corporate giving from the late 1930's to the early 1960's was accompanied by other significant economic changes. The period saw considerable growth in corporate revenues and profits and a decline in the after-tax cost or "price" of a dollar in contributions. It was also marked by related changes in corporate attitudes about the legality, appropriateness, and desirability of giving. It is the purpose of this chapter to measure, if possible, the separate contributions of each of these developments to the observed growth.

FACTORS AFFECTING CORPORATE GIVING

In the technical language of economics the effect of the level of corporation activity on the amount of giving will be described as the scale effect. The response of giving to the "price" of contributions is referred to as the price effect, and the effect of changing attitudes is described as a change in the preference or taste of corporations for giving. Problems of identifying and interpreting each of the three effects will be discussed in turn.

A convenient measure of the scale and price effects is furnished by the concept of elasticity. In this perspective, the proportionate change in giving is expressed as a ratio or percentage of the proportionate change in price or the scale of activity. If the ratio is greater than one, then giving is said to be elastic with respect to scale or price; i.e., it shows a more than proportionate response to changes in these variables. If the ratio is less than one, then giving is said to be inelastic with respect to price or scale; i.e., it shows a less than proportionate response. Measures of elasticity thus focus directly on the relative degree of responsiveness rather than on absolute change. Whenever possible, in the analysis to follow, scale and price effects will be described in terms of elasticities.

The Scale Effect

In the theory of consumer behavior, the scale effect has been associated with the relative income levels of persons or families. Viewed as a form of consumption, philanthropic giving reflects the changing composition of spending experienced by families in successively higher income levels. Higher-income families devote a higher share of income to certain kinds of services and commodities than do lower-income families, and among these services are philanthropic contributions.[1] Recent theoretical explorations have treated giving as an element in the process whereby persons seek to maximize the satisfaction (or, in economic jargon, the utility) achieved by their spending.[2] In this treatment the voluntary redistribution of income involved in giving reflects the interdependence of individual feelings of well-being. Knowledge that others are better off is a source of satisfaction. Giving, in this context, represents an activity in which people achieve satisfaction by helping to better the lot of their less fortunate neighbors.

The extension of the concept of the scale effect to corporation giving suggests that the pattern of corporate spending changes in response to increasing size of revenues and expenditures in much the same manner as that of families. This anthropomorphic view of the corporation is at sharp variance with the view that the corporation is an engine of production that arranges its inputs to production with the objective of profit-maximization. It is legitimate to regard philanthropic contributions as an input in the profit-maximizing process, in

---

[1] A number of empirical studies focusing on the relationship between the level of family income and the percentage of income "spent" on contributions have been made. Among these are ones by F. Emerson Andrews, in the *Saturday Review of Literature,* October 5, 1957; by C. Harry Kahn, *Personal Deductions in the Federal Income Tax* (Princeton, N.J.: Princeton University Press, 1960) pp. 73–87; by William Vickrey, "One Economist's View of Philanthropy," in Frank G. Dickinson, Editor, *Philanthropy and Public Policy* (New York: National Bureau of Economic Research, 1962); and by Michael Taussig, "The Charitable Contribution Deduction in the Federal Personal Income Tax" (Unpublished doctoral dissertation, Massachusetts Institute of Technology, 1965), 57–65.

[2] See, e.g., Kenneth E. Boulding, "Notes on a Theory of Philanthropy" in Dickinson, *Philanthropy and Public Policy,* pp. 67–71. Also Gary S. Becker, "Interdependent Preferences: Charity, Externalities, and Income Taxation" (Unpublished ms.).

the sense that they may directly or indirectly benefit the corporation and so contribute to long-run profits.

Although corporate giving is properly regarded as an input, there is little in the theory of the corporation to suggest what amount of giving might be optimal. It will be taken as a convenient working hypothesis that the size of giving, other factors taken into account, is proportionate to the size of corporate activity, that is, the scale elasticity of giving is one. This hypothesis will first be tested using aggregate annual data for the period 1936 to 1963. Then, later in the chapter, it will be tested by making cross-sectional analyses of giving and corporate size.

The measure of the scale of corporate activity used in the historical analysis is corporate net income after taxes. Although not wholly satisfactory in a number of respects, it probably provides as useful a measure of scale as most of the alternative measures. In scope of coverage it is coextensive with the corporate sector. Although not so good a measure as value added, income is highly correlated to that measure, and value-added data are simply not available. Sales data, for the corporate sector taken in the aggregate, are subject to serious errors of double counting, particularly over this period when the vertical relationships among corporations have undergone major changes. Finally, as pointed out in Chapter Two, both corporate and tax laws emphasize the net-income base for contributions. On these grounds, at least, income provides the operational measure of corporate size in the giving decision.

The Price Effect

The quantity of any input to production that is purchased by a corporation is determined, among other things, by its relative price. Contributions would be "purchased" in larger quantities if their price, relative to that of other inputs, is low, and in lesser quantities if their price is high. There are two dimensions to the price of corporate contributions. The first is associated with changes in the market prices of the services purchased with contributions relative to factor prices in general. The second is associated with changes in the tax rate on corporate income and so affects the net after-tax cost of a given dollar amount of contributions. Each will be examined in turn.

One can think of the contributions dollar as buying some combination of philanthropic services. With the passage of time, there may be divergent price trends for the several kinds of services included in this "market basket" of philanthropy. If the relative quantities and unit prices of philanthropic purchases were known, then, in principle, a price index for giving could be computed. This, in turn, could be related to a broader index of factor prices or possibly to an even more general price index.

The conceptual and empirical problems of devising such a price index are formidable, and in large part insoluble. For one thing, contributions are most often made for activities the value of which cannot be even approximately measured. Their value to society is felt to be high, and so they are supported despite our inability to measure them. Second, gifts are frequently made on the condition that they be matched in a specified proportion by gifts from other donors. The price to the corporation is thus lower by a factor based on the matching condition, and, to the extent that the condition evokes gifts not otherwise forthcoming, the corporation has succeeded in having more of the service produced for its given contribution.

A third difficulty relates to the degree of benefit the corporation feels it derives from contributions. If there has been a change in the degree to which contributions redound to the specific benefit of the corporation, then this may affect the company's assessment of the "quantity" of services it is able to purchase with a dollar of contributions. It may consider directly beneficial contributions as representing a higher "quantity" per dollar of outlay than those of less direct and more general benefit to the company. Fourth, changes in the "technology" of producing social welfare, health, higher education, and other services may signify lower unit prices. These are particularly difficult to measure since such changes are often accompanied by changes in the quality of the services. It is, therefore, difficult for the donor to gauge the quantity equivalent of the contributions.

The index number problem is further complicated when there are significant changes over time in the relative quantitites of the services in the market basket purchased by corporate contributions. Such changes have evidently taken place (*Table 9*). The record for the period beginning in 1936 is not available, but that for the eighteen-year period from 1947 to 1965 suggests that the corporate donations market basket has shifted increasingly to higher education and away from health and welfare.

To summarize, the value to the corporation of its purchases of philanthropic services is likely to be hard to measure. Contributions may return a benefit to the corporation only after a delay in time and

TABLE 9   Trend in the Composition of Corporate Contributions, 1947–1965

Recipient	Percentage of Contributions, Reporting Companies				
	1947	*1955*	*1959*	*1962*	*1965*
Health and welfare	66.6	50.7	45.1	40.9	41.5
(federated drives)	(37.9)	(21.9)	(25.1)	(25.5)	(24.2)
Education	13.4	31.3	39.1	41.9	38.4
Civic and cultural	20.0 {	3.2	2.9	5.3	8.6
Other		14.8	12.9	11.9	11.5
	100.0	100.0	100.0	100.0	100.0
Number of companies reporting	71	180	280	465	540
Total contributions (millions):					
Reporting companies	$16.1	$38.3	$98.6	$154.1	$209.3
All corporations	241	415	482	595	*n.a.*
Reporting companies as percentage of all	6.7	9.2	20.5	25.9	*n.a.*

NOTE: More detailed breakdowns are presented in Appendix F.
SOURCE: *Reporting Companies:* National Industrial Conference Board: *1947: The Business Record,* January, 1950, pp. 18–19; *1955: Company Contributions,* Studies In Business Policy, No. 89, 1958, p. 11; *1959: The Business Record,* June, 1961, p. 12; *1962: Business Management Record,* October, 1963, p. 25; *1965: The Conference Board Record,* October, 1966, p. 45. *All Corporations:* U.S. Treasury Department *Statistics of Income, Corporation Income Tax Returns.*

often only in a very general way. For example, contributions to higher education will result in a more highly trained labor force only after a lag of some years. Further, the corporation may directly benefit only to the degree that it succeeds in attracting the trained personnel it had a part in educating. Indeed, a recurring theme in the literature of corporate philanthropy is that, while the return to the corporation from its support of "general welfare" projects cannot be precisely measured or directly assigned, it could be substantial. By aiding scientific research, the solution of social problems, or the elevation of cultural levels, the corporation may help to produce an environment which, in a variety of ways, is congenial to its survival and prosperity.

This brings us to the second dimension to the price of corporate contributions, the significance of tax deductibility. Because contributions are most validly classed among those expenditures whose returns are deferred, uncertain, and only roughly measurable, they are more closely related to spending on, say, institutional advertising or basic research than to spending on labor, material, machinery, or direct advertising and sales campaigns. As a result, the corporate income tax rate is likely to have much greater impact on decisions about the size of contributions budgets than considerations of a price index for contributions. The longer deferred and more uncertain the return from expenditures for contributions, the more important is likely to be the immediate and certain tax saving that accompanies such expenditures, and the greater the weight given to their net after-tax cost.

Tax deductibility, therefore, is that aspect of the price of contributions included in the analysis. The price variable is defined as the net after-tax cost of a given dollar amount of contributions. For simplicity this will usually be expressed as the after-tax cost of one dollar in contributions. This is the same as the complement of the marginal tax rate expressed in percentage form.

The "price" of giving, so defined, is not the same for all corporations, since corporations may fall into income classes that place them in one of several marginal tax-rate brackets. The $495 million in corporate contributions for 1953, for example, was made by corporations paying one of four separate "prices" for their contributions. For companies with negative net income (or net loss) for the year, the price of $1.00 in contributions was $1.00, their marginal tax rate being zero.[3] For profitable corporations having less than $25,000 in net income, the price was $0.70, their marginal tax rate being 30 per cent. For those having more than $25,000 in net income but not subject to the excess-profits tax, the price was $0.48, and for those subject to the excess-profits tax it was $0.18.

Unfortunately, the Internal Revenue Service tabulations do not present data on gifts and contributions by income classes and so one cannot know how many dollars of contributions were made at each of the several "prices." For this reason it is not possible to compute a precise measure of the average "price" of contributions. A rough measure of the downward trend in "price" over this period of rising tax rates is presented in Table 10 below; the construction of this measure and an evaluation of assumptions and biases are described in Appendix Table VII. For most years the average "price" is the complement of the ordinary corporate income tax rate, as this is the "price" faced by corporations that accounted for the preponderance of corporate net income and contributions. In ten of the twenty-eight years some—but probably not complete—account is taken of the fact that a large part of corporate net income was earned by corporations

---

[3] The price would be $1.00 for many corporations only through 1954. After 1954, a contributions deduction greater than 5 per cent of income could be carried forward for two years, to be offset against income in those years. Thus, only if a corporation had losses for three consecutive years would the "price" be 100 per cent of the contribution.

subject to the excess-profits tax, and who thereby faced a much lower "price" of giving.

Beginning in the late 1930's, when the "price" of $1.00 in contribution was first 85 cents and then 81 cents for most contributions, the "price" has shown a strong downward trend. The trend has not been a regular one, however. In the six excess-profits tax years spanning World War II, the "price" was sharply lower, reaching a low point of 28 cents in 1943. This period was followed by a four-year plateau in corporate income tax rates, during which the "price" of most contributions was 62 cents. The four excess-profits tax years spanning the Korean War produced a second sharp dip in the "price" of contributions. This then was followed by a ten-year plateau in corporate tax rates, from 1954 through 1963, during which the "price" of most contributions was 48 cents.[4]

This pattern may make it difficult to separate the price effect from the effect of the time trend in the preference for giving. It is possible that the rise in giving as a percentage of income, as described in Chapter Two, was in part the result of a ratchet process. In this process, the stimulus to giving produced by high excess-profits tax rates may have led corporations to make larger commitments to donees— commitments, which, once tax rates were lowered, were hard to reduce, but which were less burdensome to maintain than would have been the case had the "price" been restored to its pre-excess-profits tax level. If so, then what may appear to have been the pure effect of an upward trend in tastes may in reality have been partly a price effect. One may perhaps take comfort from the fact that the role of price in the development of tastes is a ubiquitous one, and so the problem is not unique to philanthropic contributions.

The Trend in Tastes and Other
Influences on Giving

As mentioned in Chapter Two, there appears to have been a considerable liberalization over the period in corporate attitudes toward the

---

[4] Technically, some of the contributions made during 1963 were made at a higher "price," as corporation income tax rates were reduced effective January 1, 1964. However, only a small part of corporate net income was reported by corporations whose accounting year ended after December 31, 1963, i.e., between January 1, and June 30, 1964. The *Statistics of Income* for 1963 included all corporations whose accounting year ended between July 1, 1963 and June 30, 1964. In addition, since the tax rate was, in effect, an average based on the number of days the company operated under the old higher and new lower tax rates, the "price" change for any given corporation could only have been very minor, at most half of the 2 per cent increase for corporations whose accounting year ended June 30, 1964.

legality, appropriateness, and desirability of giving. Precise measures of the effects of this change on corporate behavior do not exist. However, the subject has received sufficient attention and discussion to warrant an attempt to determine whether it has made a significant difference in giving levels.

Affecting any inclination toward philanthropic giving on the part of corporation management is its awareness of the legal right of corporations to make contributions. Liberalization of this legal right in all likelihood reflected successful efforts by a number of corporations whose attitudes toward giving had changed. This in turn led to a more general corporate awareness of this right, which then may have played an expanded role in what we have chosen to call a change in preference or taste for giving.

Before 1936, common law precedents were few and presented little clear guidance whether or to what a corporation might make donations.[5] Specific state laws permitting corporations to make contributions did give explicit recognition to the right, but, before 1935, only seven states had enacted such laws. The Federal Revenue Act of 1935, which permitted deduction of contributions up to 5 per cent of income, probably gave support to a broader interpretation of existing state laws by designating contributions as a category of tax-deductible outlay separate and distinct from business expenses.[6]

As of 1940, only nine states had permissive legislation, the main pressure toward greater state permissiveness coming with World War II. By 1952 statutes permitting corporate giving had been enacted in 29 states and Hawaii,[7] and by 1959 this number had grown to 41.[8]

Liberalization of state laws was accompanied by more permissive interpretation by courts. Probably the most significant decision in this respect was that rendered in the case of a manufacturing company which made a $1,500-gift to Princeton University. In finding in favor of the corporation, and against the shareholders who had brought suit, the decision held that the boards of corporations may contribute for purposes which, in their judgment:

> Will conduce to the betterment of social and economic conditions, thereby permitting such corporations, as creatures of the State, to dis-

---

[5] F. Emerson Andrews, *Corporation Giving* (New York: Russell Sage Foundation, 1952), pp. 229–233.

[6] *Ibid.*, pp. 233–239.

[7] *Ibid.*

[8] Bert S. Prunty, Jr., "Love and the Corporation," *Virginia Law Review*, April, 1960, p. 469.

charge their obligations to society while, at the same time, reaping the benefits which essentially accrue to them through public recognition of their existence within the economic and social, as well as within the legal, structure of society.[9]

To measure the effects of attitudinal change as separate from, though partly determined by, change in legal status, one ideally ought to have an independent and direct measure of attitudes, over time, and comparable from one period to the next. Unfortunately no data exist that would permit the construction of such a series. While the literature does not lend itself to the quantification of an index of taste or preference, a sampling might suggest something of the direction it has taken.

The general trend in corporate attitudes is summed up by the 1952 testimony of Frank W. Abrams, former Chairman of the Board of Standard Oil Company (New Jersey), in the A. P. Smith Case:

> During the forty years of my business career, I have observed a slow but steady transition in the attitude of corporate management from one of more or less exclusive preoccupation with self-interest to one of self-interest tempered with a broadening sense of social consciousness.

This more general attitude has been refined by a number of persons, perhaps most notably by W. Homer Turner, Executive Director of the United States Steel Foundation, and by Richard Eells. In a 1961 statement, Eells, who has written widely on the social and political rationale of corporate giving, made the case as follows:

> Every company—large or small—has an obligation to its shareholders, and to all the other interests it is bound to protect. Therefore it should use its support program as an instrument of corporate survival in a free society. . . . The major function of corporate giving . . . is to vitalize the defenses of a free society by active support of those private sectors that invigorate freedom.[10]

A more contemporary statement, reflecting the further development and enlargement of corporate attitudes is that by Dr. Frank Stanton, President of Columbia Broadcasting System, in Feburary, 1967, before the Arts Council of Columbus, Ohio. Dr. Stanton pointed to the sharply increased corporate support of higher education as in-

---

[9] A. P. Smith Mfg. Co. & Barlow, et al. 26 New Jersey Super. 106 (1953).
[10] *The Changing Role of American Corporate Philanthropy*, Report on Midwest Public Relations Conference, University of Wisconsin, October 10, 1961 (Madison: University of Wisconsin Press, 1962), p. 16.

dicative of business' "broadened horizons and increased awareness [of the fact that] business is learning, along with every other sector of society . . . that it both nourishes and is nourished by all those other activities that give any society character, richness, variety and meaning." He asked whether the arts might not be "ultimately the meeting ground where liberal education and progressive business come together." Feeling that the arts might be the first place in which the vitality of individualism might be lost, he suggested that, "if this were to happen, no liberal education will save our kind of society and no business enterprise will long endure in what is left of it."

The liberalization of corporate attitudes toward giving, and its acceptance as a legitimate corporate function, is reflected in formalized policy-making and administration by increasing numbers of companies. Referring to his National Industrial Conference Board surveys of corporation giving patterns, John H. Watson III reported:

> In 1955, it was difficult to locate as many as 15 company policy statements on contributions during a nation-wide survey. During a 1965 statistical survey, however, copies of 45 policies were submitted to the Board without special request. . . .
>
> Today, between one-fourth and one-third of those companies having contribution programs have also established contribution committees, and thereby tie in contribution objectives with overall company goals. . . .
>
> The staff concerned, on a full-time basis, with the giving function is now larger than ever before. One-third of the 55 members on The Conference Board's Council of Executives on Company Contributions today spends a majority or virtually all of their time on the function. And among the larger companies represented in NICB surveys, two-thirds use a contribution budget.[11]

Finally, mention should be made of less obvious, but nonetheless significant, pressures to contribute that have been brought to bear upon executives. One observer has identified two principal kinds; the first is described as "executive backscratching," and the second as pressures from government, particularly in the 1960's. He doubts, however, that companies often respond to such importuning if they do not see the social value of the suggested projects.

An attempt was made to measure the effect of attitudes toward giving through the use of a proxy variable. This variable was simply a series of successive integers from 1 through 28, assigned to the suc-

---

[11] "Recent Company Contribution Trends," *The Conference Board Record*, National Industrial Conference Board, January, 1968, p. 4.

cessive years of the period, 1936 having a value of 1; 1963, a value of 28. Technically, this variable is a proxy for the effects of all long-run changes other than those specifically included in the analysis. Tastes are presumably, but not certainly, the most important of these other changes. If there were any other developments that took place in a relatively persistent and progressive pattern over the period, the trend variable would serve as a proxy for them also. Although no other such developments are apparent, it should be kept in mind that the trend variable may measure the influence of factors as yet unrecognized.

Anticipation of Tax Rate Changes

An additional explanatory variable was included in the analysis. This was a number that reflected the expectation that an excess-profits tax would be either enacted or repealed in the following year. If it were widely anticipated that this tax would be enacted, bringing with it a sharp reduction in the net after-tax cost of giving, corporations might defer gifts planned for the current year, give more the following year, and thus enjoy a reduction, over-all, in the after-tax cost of their giving. On the other hand, if a repeal of the excess-profits tax were widely anticipated, then corporations might move next year's planned giving ahead into the current year, while the cost of giving was still low. As will be shown in Chapter Four, the existence of company-sponsored foundations probably facilitated such responses. Serving as reservoirs into which contributions could be poured or from which they could be drained, these foundations made it possible for corporations to maintain a more uniform flow of contributions to their ultimate beneficiaries, while taking advantage of tax-savings in the timing of their deductions for contributions.

Inspection of the time series of corporate contributions suggests that this pattern of behavior took place. The excess-profits tax rate was sharply increased in 1940, and gifts from corporations with profits increased from $29 million in 1939 to $37 million in 1940. The tax was repealed in 1946, and gifts dropped from an unusually high 1945 total of $263 million to an unusually low 1946 total of $211 million. This came after seven successive annual increases since 1938. In 1947 gifts rose again to $238 million, a level more in line with their secular growth pattern. An excess-profits tax was again imposed in 1950, and gifts rose from an unusually low level of $220 million in 1949 to $250 million in 1950. The tax was repealed in 1954, and gifts dropped from an extremely high $491 million in 1953 to a very low $309 million in 1954. They returned to $410 million in 1955, slightly above their 1952 level of $396 million.

In the time-series analysis, the tax-change anticipations effect is measured through the use of a proxy variable (*Table 10*). The variable is assigned a value of one in all years except those adjacent to the enactment or repeal of the excess-profits tax. The variable was assigned a value of zero for the year preceding an enactment or following a repeal of the tax. It was assigned a value of two for the first year the tax was in effect after enactment and the last year it was in effect before its repeal. Although this treatment was rather crude, it was felt that, for present purposes, little would be gained from a more elaborate treatment.

The effect of expectations about the excess-profits tax probably should be regarded mainly as an irregular factor, unrelated to the longer-run forces making for permanent changes in the level of giving. The variable was included in the analysis principally to discount its influence, in order to measure the effects of the other variables more precisely.

The Profitability Effect

A corporation's disposition to make contributions is associated not only with the quantity of profits from which contributions might be drawn, but also with the rate of return on shareholders' investment, i.e., profits as a percentage of the corporation's net worth. The higher the profit rate, with all other factors equal, the more disposed will be the corporation's managers toward distributing a larger-than-normal share of profits to philanthropy. The converse applies for low profit rates. Profit rates move with the level or scale of profits, and so one would expect to find measured scale and profitability effects to be fairly similar in value. However, because shareholders' investment also changes over time, a given movement in profitability is not exactly proportional to that in profits. The difference in movements reflect the profitability effect.

To isolate the effect of profitability on contributions, net worth was included as a separate variable in the analysis. This was done in preference to using the ratio of profits to net worth as an explicit profitability variable.[12] Movements in net income, holding net worth con-

---

[12] An important reason for adopting this treatment was to avoid the high intercorrelation which would exist between the profits (or scale) variable and the profitability variable, the latter being a fraction with profits as its numerator. This intercorrelation would complicate the interpretation of the regressions.

stant, represent like movements in the rate of return on investment. Therefore, the coefficient of the income variable, in equations also containing the net-worth variable, measures the response of contributions to changes in the rate of profit.

The net-worth variable used in the analysis was that for all net-income corporations as presented in *Statistics of Income*. It is on a book-value basis since it is derived from the balance sheet data provided on corporation income tax returns, and reflects the accounting conventions applied in determining income subject to tax. These data were deflated by the implicit price deflator for the gross national product, as were the contributions and income data. As will be seen below, the net-worth data have shortcomings which may seriously limit the significance of findings based on their use, although the biases are capable of at least crude evaluation.

TIME-SERIES ANALYSIS

Table 10 summarizes the aforementioned variables chosen to analyze the movement in contributions, and presents the annual data on which the analysis is based. The techniques of multiple regression analysis were used to describe the several relationships. In addition to relating contributions to the income (scale), price, trend, tax-change expectations, and profitability of the current year, they were also related to income (scale) and price of the preceding year. It was found that the current-year-only regressions contained significant levels of serial correlation, which were reduced to nonsignificant levels by the introduction of lagged price and income. The combined effects of current- and preceding-year price or income, keeping in mind their intercorrelations, could be interpreted as elasticities.[13]

The regressions were run in sequence, beginning with one explanatory variable and successively adding additional explanatory variables. Attention was focused on those changes in regression coefficients which helped to determine whether the coefficient measured only the relationship between giving and the variable in question or whether the variable indirectly reflected the effect of other variables with which it was correlated. The variables, with the exception of

---

[13] The inclusion of the lagged income and price variables meant that the regression analysis was based on 27 instead of 28 observations, the current-year data for 1936 being omitted. Although data for 1964 has become available since the 1936–1963 regressions were run, it was decided, because of time factors, not to recompute the regressions to include 1964 data. As will be shown below, it is doubtful that the addition of these data would have changed the results in any significant way.

TABLE 10   Contributions of Net-Income Corporations and Related Economic Variables Used to Explain Their Behavior, 1936–1963
(Dollar values in millions of 1936 dollars)

Year	Gifts and Contributions	Net Income After Taxes, Before Gifts and Contributions	"Price" of $1 in Contributions	Trend	Expectation of Tax Change	Net Worth
1936	$ 27.0	$ 8,594	$0.850	1	1	$111,338
1937	27.8	8,288	0.850	2	1	108,351
1938	22.4	5,765	0.810	3	1	96,842
1939	28.7	7,772	0.810	4	0	109,039
1940	36.0	8,696	0.585	5	2	113,066
1941	51.6	10,162	0.322	6	1	115,542
1942	77.4	9,820	0.323	7	1	105,707
1943	118.8	9,927	0.283	8	1	104,733
1944	170.9	9,269	0.290	9	1	106,346
1945	188.1	8,410	0.336	10	2	103,404
1946	135.1	12,038	0.620	11	0	95,157
1947	136.2	13,145	0.620	12	1	97,074
1948	126.6	13,377	0.620	13	1	101,140
1949	118.8	11,531	0.620	14	2	105,397
1950	133.1	14,675	0.398	15	2	114,864
1951	170.1	12,088	0.327	16	1	114,402
1952	193.3	10,900	0.355	17	1	117,116
1953	237.4	11,162	0.360	18	2	120,285
1954	147.3	11,425	0.480	19	0	120,556
1955	192.6	14,188	0.480	20	1	133,970
1956	187.6	13,860	0.480	21	1	138,293
1957	180.5	13,081	0.480	22	1	135,700
1958	163.5	11,353	0.480	23	1	140,757
1959	198.4	13,174	0.480	24	1	149,103
1960	196.4	12,779	0.480	25	1	151,792
1961	206.1	13,479	0.480	26	1	158,868
1962	238.4	14,613	0.480	27	1	167,665
1963	259.6	15,758	0.480	28	1	175,725

trend and tax-change expectations, were expressed in logarithmic form so the regression coefficients could be directly read as measures of elasticity. The sequences of equations and tables of simple correlations among the several variables are presented in Appendix C.

The equations selected as most clearly significant are presented in Table 11. As mentioned above, income and price for both the current and preceding year were included among the explanatory variables. The equations in Appendix C show that the current year's income generally had much more significant regression coefficients than did the income of the preceding year. Because of the high correlation between the two measures, only current-year income was included as the income variable in the first of each pair of equations in Table 11. By

TABLE 11   Relationships Between Corporation Giving and Explanatory Variables

Dependent Variable	Constant Term	Scale and Profitability Elasticity Coefficients[a]	Price Elasticity Coefficients[b]	Expectations (E) or Net-Worth (NW) Coefficients	Trend Coefficients	Adjusted R-Squared	Von Neumann Ratio
SCALE VARIANT							
$\log GC =$	-0.75	$+1.05 \log Y$ (4.08)[c]	$-1.03 \log P_{t-1}$ (9.08)	$+0.055$ E (1.96)	$+0.016$ T (4.83)	0.93	1.48
$\log GC =$	-2.44	$+0.97 \log Y$ (3.65) $+0.46 \log Y_{t-1}$ (1.72)	$+0.34 \log P$ (1.58) $-1.26 \log P_{t-1}$ (6.59)	$+0.078$ E (2.44)	$+0.012$ T (3.32)	0.94	1.93
PROFITABILITY VARIANT							
$\log GC =$	$+6.01$	$+0.81 \log Y$ (3.17)	$-0.90 \log P_{t-1}$ (7.86)	$-1.20 \log$ NW (2.81)	$+0.029$ T (5.24)	0.94	2.64
$\log GC =$	$+7.33$	$+0.66 \log Y$ (2.46) $+0.04 \log Y_{t-1}$ (0.14)	$-0.28 \log P$ (1.30) $-0.66 \log P_{t-1}$ (2.99)	$-1.48 \log$ NW (2.68)	$+0.033$ T (4.03)	0.94	2.26

[a] Coefficient of simple correlation between $\log Y$ and $\log Y_{t-1} = +0.77$.
[b] Coefficient of simple correlation between $\log P$ and $\log P_{t-1} = +0.78$.
[c] T-ratios in parentheses.

contrast, the preceding-year's price was found to have much more significant regression coefficients than current-year price and, again because of the high intercorrelation, only it was included. For purposes of comparison, equations including both current and lagged income and price variables are also presented.

Scale and Profitability Elasticities

Table 11 tends to confirm the expectation that the scale elasticity of giving has a value close to unity. In the first equation the elasticity of giving with respect to the current-year's income was +1.05. Although the second equation yields an elasticity of +0.81, there is some reason to believe that it is understated. Because the second equation includes net worth as a separate variable, the regression coefficient for the income variable measures the effect of profitability instead of the pure effect of income or scale. Income and net worth move together, and the intercorrelation is high enough ($r = +.6$) so that some of the purely scale effects may have been reflected in the coefficient of the net-worth variable.

On somewhat different grounds, the net-worth effect may be overstated (and the scale effect understated) because errors in the net-worth measure probably lead to an understatement of its true variability.[14] This produces a higher measure of net-worth elasticity and a correspondingly lower measure of income elasticity.[15] It is of interest to note that the observed income elasticity (+0.81) is about as far below unity as the net-worth elasticity (−1.20) is above unity. One can only speculate about how much closer together these might be brought if a more adequate measure of net worth had been available. The negative sign of the net-worth coefficient is what one would ex-

---

[14] Reasons for the understatement are related to change in the accounting treatment of corporate assets over the period and to the use of the gross national product implicit deflator to put the net -worth data on a constant-dollar basis. The basic net-worth data are those contained in the United States Internal Revenue Service's *Statistics of Income*. They are on a book-value basis and, over the period, probably increasingly reflect historical cost valuation. Inventory valuation has increasingly reflected the wider use of Last In–First Out cost accounting, and depreciation policies have increasingly emphasized accelerated depreciation patterns. The use of a price deflator based on current-year product prices, when applied to asset data containing fixed assets of varying ages and costs of acquisition, probably leads to overdeflation. Both biases lead to an understatement of the growth and variability of the net-worth series.

[15] For a discussion of the statistical basis for this evaluation of effects of bias, see Mordecai Ezekiel and Karl Fox, *Methods of Correlation and Regression Analysis*, 3rd edition (New York: John Wiley & Sons, 1959), pp. 311–317.

pect. That is, the larger the shareholders' investment, net income being held constant, the lower the rate of return and the lower the giving rate.

The scale variant equation, containing both current- and preceding-year income, also suggests that the scale elasticity is close to unity. Although the two regression coefficients add to considerably more than unity (1.43), when the relatively high intercorrelation ($r = +.77$) is considered, the "net" scale effect is well below the total. In summary, the findings suggest that, when other factors are taken into account, the growth in the scale of corporate activity as reflected by income has tended to increase giving in the same proportion. For an explanation of the rise in the ratio of giving to income over the period, the effects of other factors will have to be examined.

Examination of the income coefficients in two equations in the profitability variant of the analysis suggests a profitability elasticity of less than unity. However, as mentioned above, it is difficult to separate profitability from scale effects; this problem is compounded by deficiencies in data, particularly in the net-worth variable. Differences in regression coefficients for the income variable between the scale and profitability variants might be taken as reflecting the profitability effect. These differences suggest that the effect is not large.

Perhaps a low profitability effect is what one might expect. Corporations might regard periods of high or low profit rates as basically temporary departures from their normal or long-run rates, and giving might be related more to the long-run than to the current rate. It could likewise be argued that giving might be related more to the long-run than to the current absolute amount of net income. However, corporate decisions might be more directly affected by the amount of profits presently available for distribution than by the rate of return on investment that these profits signified. This would be the case, for example, in corporations that have adopted a policy of giving a more or less constant percentage of profits. Such rule-of-thumb calculations may be fairly important, if not explicitly stated, in many corporate-giving decisions.

Price Elasticity

The regressions indicate that giving responded to changes in the marginal tax rate (complement), which affected the immediate after-tax cost or "price" of making gifts. Moreover, the response appeared to be proportionate to the relative change in price, the elasticity coefficients having values ranging near −1.0. As shown in Appendix Table XI, price elasticity measures were only slightly affected by the addition of explanatory variables other than price, suggesting that the coefficients were fairly pure measures of the price effect. Moreover, taken separately, the two price coefficients exhibited very high degrees of statistical significance.

What was unexpected in the analysis of the price effect was the very significant relationship found between giving in one year and the price in the preceding year. Also unexpected was the degree to which the introduction of preceding-year price reduced the effect of current-year price. As mentioned above, each measure of price, taken separately, showed an elasticity of close to −1.0, and was statistically significant. However, when both price measures were included in the regression, the elasticity coefficient for the current-year's price fell to a low value, was as often positive as negative, and, in all cases, was not statistically significant. By contrast, the elasticity coefficient for the preceding-year's price retained a value near −1.0, and in all cases remained highly significant.[16]

The greater significance of preceding-year over current-year price regressions may in part reflect the introduction of the tax-change expectations variable into the analysis. As one would expect, the four episodic movements in tax-change expectations were accompanied by large concurrent (and opposite) changes in price. The expectations variable was thus more highly correlated with current-year price ($r = −.373$) than with preceding-year price ($r = −.034$). The current-year price variable in equations also containing the preceding-year price variable had positive regression coefficients only when the expectations variable was included in the equation.[17]

This pattern may be seen in Table 11. In the scale variant equation, which contains the tax-change expectation variable, the current-year price regression coefficient is positive (+.34). In the profitability variant equation, which does not contain the tax-change expectations variable, the current-year price coefficient is negative (−.28). In

---

[16] One other effect of the inclusion of preceding-year price in the regression was to remove the serial correlation present in all of the regressions in which this variable was not included.

[17] This statement is based on those equations which demonstrated no significant degree of serial correlation at the 5 per cent level of significance (*see Appendix Table XI*).

both equations the coefficients of the current- and preceding-year price variables add to a negative value slightly below one.

The precise mechanism by which the price effect results from the joint operation of current- and preceding-year prices evades simple explanation, and the correlation analysis is too broad to describe the pattern of this process. The broad findings, however, do suggest a price elasticity of giving somewhere near minus one. In this, the findings are in general accord with what the earlier discussion implied about this price elasticity.

To summarize, like other inputs to production, the quantity of contributions purchased is determined by the benefits that the corporation feels it derives from them. However, the projection of the return from philanthropic outlays is especially subject to problems of futurity and uncertainty, and so the immediate and certain tax savings that accompany contributions are likely to weigh more heavily in the decision. The observed elasticity coefficients suggest that tax savings have, in fact, weighed heavily in decisions to give.

Expectations of Changes in
Excess-Profits Taxes

The variable depicting expectations of changes in the excess-profits tax shows a positive and statistically significant effect on gifts and contributions. As shown above in Table 10, the values given in this variable are arbitrary. They do not attempt to describe the intensity or consensus of expectations, which may have varied from one war-time period to another. Nonetheless, this variable was found to have some separate significance, which would seem to justify its inclusion in the analysis. Moreover, despite the possibility that this variable has made it more difficult to isolate current- and preceding-year price effects, it probably has led to less ambiguous measures of the income, price, and trend effects.

Trend in Tastes and Other Influences
on Giving

The separate effect of progressive changes in "other" factors, as reflected by the trend variable, was found to be substantial and statistically significant. There were, of course, high positive correlations of the trend variable with the giving, income, and net-worth variables, and a moderate negative correlation with the price variable. However, in the multiple regression equations, where the net effects of each variable were separately measured, the trend variable exhibited consistently high and significant values. This indicates that the passage of time, and the developments associated with it other than those mentioned above, made an important independent contribution to the growth in giving.

The regression equations in which the net effect of the trend are most clearly measured are those showing the least evidence of serial correlation. The eight equations having nonsignificant Von Neumann ratios (5-per-cent level of significance) are presented in Appendix Table XII. The T-ratio for the trend variable for these equations in all cases was statistically significant, ranging in value from 3.32 to 9.99. The compound annual percentage rate of growth indicated by the regression coefficient ranged from 2.8 per cent to 8.1 per cent, with a median value of 5.7 per cent.[18] This suggests that, over the twenty-seven-year period, factors other than income and price were responsible for a more than 300 per cent increase in gifts and contributions.

These findings lend support to the argument that changes in corporate attitudes toward giving played a major role in its growth over the period. The attitude changes reflected in the statements of corporate officials cited above on pages 44 through 47 apparently represented much more than lip service to worthy goals. Such stated attitudes, progressively more receptive to notions of the legality, desirability, and appropriateness of giving, appear to have been accompanied by an equally strong change in corporate behavior.[19]

While attitudinal change may have been a major proximate cause of the growth in giving, it, in turn, may have reflected a number of indirect developments that showed progressive change over the period. Some of these developments, particularly of a legal and social nature, have been mentioned above. Another one that comes to mind is the increased governmental support of public higher education, which

---

[18] As presented in Appendix Table XII, the regression coefficients of the trend variable ranged in value from .012 to .034. The coefficient represents the year-to-year change in the logarithm $_{10}$ of giving, other variables held constant. Expressed as antilogs, the coefficient is thus equivalent to the ratio of giving in a particular year to that in the preceding year. This ratio is the same as one plus the annual compound growth rate expressed in decimal form.

[19] A comparison of the findings of this time-series analysis with one conducted independently by another researcher is presented in Appendix E. Both are based on essentially the same data and method, but with significant differences in data treatment. The comparison reveals more fully the reasons the particular data treatment here adopted produces less ambiguous measures of the effects being examined.

TABLE 12 1963 to 1964 Change in Contributions, Corporate Income, and Price, Corporations with Net Income
(Dollar values in millions of 1936 dollars)

	1963	*1964*	*Percentage Change*
Gifts and contributions	$ 259.6	$ 283.5	+9.2
Net income after taxes, before gifts and contributions	15,758	18,103	+14.9
Net after-tax cost or "price" of $1 in contributions	0.48	0.50	+4.2

may have had an indirect effect on the increased corporate support of private colleges and universities. Certainly, the argument that private higher education must remain strong to provide balance, innovation, and variety in higher education, in the face of rapidly expanding public programs, has figured prominently in fund-raising appeals.

Changes from 1963 to 1964

As mentioned above in note 13, data on 1964 corporate giving, income, and tax rates became available shortly before the final editorial revisions were made in the text and well after the regression analysis had been made. It was possible to include the 1964 data in the descriptive sections of the study, and in the statistical appendixes, but not in the regressions.

To determine whether the inclusion of 1964 data in the regressions would have materially changed them, comparisons of 1964 to 1963 variables are presented in Table 12. The percentage change in gifts and contributions (+9.2) is somewhat less than the combined effect of scale (income) and price, which, if elasticities of, respectively, plus-one and minus-one are assumed, would predict an increase in gifts and contributions of 10.1 per cent.[20]

One reason for the lower realized increase in gifts and contributions may have been expectations of the tax reduction in 1964. This may have led some corporations to move some of their giving ahead into 1963, thus making for a lower 1963–1964 increase. However, the "price" change was not large. In any event the 1963–1964 patterns of change are sufficiently close to those described by the 1936–1963 regressions to reassure one that, were 1964 data included in the regres-

---

[20] This is the product of the percentage change in income and price, computed as follows (1 +.149) x (1 −.042) which equals 1.101 or, in percentage terms, 100 per cent plus 10.1 per cent.

sions, the findings would have been substantially the same as those presented in Table 11.

CROSS-SECTIONAL ANALYSIS

The cross-sectional examination of corporate data was made to illuminate influences on corporate contributions that are not directly measurable in time-series analysis. These include the relationship between giving and such things as the size of corporations, their individual profitability, and the degree of capital- or labor-intensive production. Not measurable were the effects of such time-related factors as changes in tax rates ("price") and in the propensity to give.

As in the time-series analysis, the technique of multiple correlation was employed. Data were assembled for 121 industry classes in manufacturing, as presented by the Internal Revenue Service in the *Source Book* for its *Statistics of Income*.[21] The financial statements for 1954–1957 were combined to minimize the distortion contained in data for only one year. The period spans virtually the whole business cycle that had its initial trough in August, 1954, its peak in July, 1957, and its final trough in April, 1958.[22] As the contributions, profits, dividends, etc. of the several industries are affected in different degrees through the cycle, a full cycle was used to minimize what, for present purposes, would be spurious variation in the data.

The analysis was limited to the relatively homogeneous manufacturing sector because it was felt that intersectoral differences might obscure the effects of the variables examined if the other industrial sectors were covered. Not only were the corporations in the manufacturing sector somewhat alike with respect to their production operations, but there was a large enough number of industries (121) on which to base the statistical analysis.

Some notion of the variety among sectors is given in Table 13. Here it can be seen, first, that there was a large variation in the size of corporations (as roughly measured by average annual income). Average annual income ranged from $5 thousand for corporations in the service industries to $182 million for those in manufacturing. In addi-

---

[21] The *Source Book* contains balance sheets and income statements for more detailed industry categories than those published in the *Statistics of Income*. The *Source Book* was generously made available to the National Bureau by the Internal Revenue Service.

[22] More exactly, the period includes the four returns filed by corporations having tax years ending on July 1, 1954, through June 30, 1958. As calendar-year filing is the most common period adopted by corporations, it is both substantially correct and descriptively convenient to designate the period in calendar years.

TABLE 13 Gifts and Contributions as Percentage of Corporate Income and of Distribution of Corporate Income, All Corporations and Eight Major Industrial Sectors, 1954–1957

	Average Annual Before-Tax Income per Corporation (in thousands)	Gifts and Contribution as Percentage of:			
		Corporate Income		Distributions of Income Measured as:	
		Before Tax	After Tax	Contributions and Dividends	Contributions, Officers' Compensation, and Dividends
All corporations	$ 56.4	0.88	1.61	2.77	1.59
Agriculture, forestry, and fisheries	13.1	0.98	2.09	2.50	0.87
Mining, quarrying	96.5	0.66	1.52	0.85	0.73
Construction	14.2	1.67	3.40	10.68	1.31
Manufacturing	181.6	0.96	1.94	3.14	2.10
Public utilities	177.8	0.51	1.04	1.14	0.98
Trade	18.1	1.42	2.80	6.21	1.61
Finance, insurance, and real estate	38.5	0.52	0.68	1.87	1.17
Services	5.0	1.56	3.25	6.02	1.25

SOURCE: U.S. Internal Revenue Service, *Statistics of Income, 1954, 1955, 1956–7, 1957–8,* pp. 44–51, 31–38, 25–32, and 31–38, respectively.

tion, there was great variation in the percentage of income distributed as gifts and contributions. Measured relative to after-tax income, this percentage ranged from 0.68 per cent for the finance, insurance, and real estate sector to 3.40 per cent for construction.[23]

The basic data used in the correlation analysis were first converted to logarithmic form. This was done so that the calculated relationships between giving and the several explanatory variables could be interpreted as measures of elasticity. Estimating equations containing from one to six independent variables were computed (*see Table 14*).[24] Table 14 includes the T-ratios of the regression coefficients so that the statistical significance of each variable may be assessed. The relationship of each variable to contributions will be discussed in turn.

Corporate Size

An aspect of corporate giving that has received some attention is the broad empirical finding that, as corporate size increases, the percentage of income given declines. The pattern was described for 1948 by F. Emerson Andrews, who offered the following rather striking comparison: "The 601 giant corporations [over $100 million in assets] appear to have given in 1948 only one-quarter as much of their profits as the half million corporations with assets below $1 million."[25] A parallel tabulation for 1957 reveals much the same relationship (*Column 7 in Table 15*). Taken at face value, these findings imply that the largest corporations are less generous, relative to their income available for giving, than are the small ones.

This finding is particularly surprising in the light of what is known

---

[23] The meaning of the income measure itself is subject to interpretation. As will be shown later in detail, the accounting measure of income as provided in corporate income tax returns may not be fully equivalent to the return to invested capital as usually conceived. For example, some of this return may be found in the compensation of the company's officers, whose salaries may contain elements of return on capital. When contributions are related to distributions of income, under the alternative assumptions that officers' compensation is or is not a distribution of income (rather than a payment for labor services), the ratios of contributions to income for the seven major sectors are significantly reordered (*Table 13*).

[24] Of the six explanatory variables used in the multiple correlation, five were taken from the *Source Book* for *Statistics of Income*, cited above. One, employment, is derived from the periodic *Census of Manufactures*, and so is available for 1954 only; U.S. Bureau of the Census, *Census of Manufacturers, 1954*, Volume I: *Summary Statistics*, Chapter IV, pp. 204–1 through 204–23. The matrix of simple correlation coefficients underlying Table 14 is presented in Appendix D. A seventh variable, net income after taxes, was originally included in the analysis. It was not included in Table 14 because, in the cross-sectional data in which tax rates were substantially equal for all corporations, it 'was very highly correlated with before-tax income.

[25] F. Emerson Andrews, *Corporation Giving*, Table 4, pp. 44–45.

TABLE 14 Regression Equations Relating Corporation Giving to Successively Larger Numbers of Explanatory Variables, Logarithmically Transformed[a] (Cross-sectional data)

Equation	Constant Term	Number of Corporations	Income	Net Worth	Employment	Officers' Compensation	Dividends	Coefficient of Multiple Determination (R^2)
A	$X_1 =$ 481,397	$+$ .549 X_2						.225
B	$X_1 =$ 10,747	$+$ .231 X_2	$+$ .675 X_3					.636
C	$X_1 =$ −11,447	$+$ .223 X_2	$+$ .517 X_3	$+$ .171 X_4				.642
D	$X_1 =$ −86,471	$+$ .127 X_2	$+$ .470 X_3	$+$ .105 X_4	$+$ .266 X_5			.663
E	$X_1 =$ 49,054	$+$ .504 X_2	$+$ .418 X_3	$+$ .366 X_4	$+$ .270 X_5	$-$ .591 X_6		.730
F	$X_1 =$ 99,357	$+$ .423 X_2	$+$ .111 X_3	$-$ .210 X_4	$+$ .210 X_5	$-$ .253 X_6	$+$ .709 X_7	.837
T-Ratios								
A		5.880						
B		3.304	11.536					
C		3.197	4.136	1.423				
D		1.645	3.815	0.875	2.679			
E		5.096	3.766	3.090	3.020	5.341		
F		5.445	1.181	1.852	3.009	2.671	8.681	

[a] Based on cross-sectional data for 121 manufacturing industries for the four-year period, 1954–1957.

Definitions of the variables presented in the above table:

$X_1 =$ Total Gifts and Contributions of Corporations in the Industry, 1954–1957 (Log_{10}).
$X_2 =$ Number of Corporations in the Industry, 1954–1957 (Log_{10}).
$X_3 =$ Total Compiled Net Profit Before Taxes, Corporations in the Industry, 1954–1957 (Log_{10}).
$X_4 =$ Total Net Worth of Corporations in the Industry, 1954–1957 (Log_{10}).
$X_5 =$ Employment in Manufacturing Establishments Classified in Industry, 1954 (Log_{10}).
$X_6 =$ Officers Compensation of Corporations in the Industry, 1954–1957 (Log_{10}).
$X_7 =$ Total Dividends Paid, Corporations in the Industry, 1954–1957 (Log_{10}).

TABLE 15 Gifts and Contributions as Percentage of Corporate Income Variously Defined, and Sales, by Size of Assets, Active Corporations, 1957

Asset Size Class	Dollar Values (Millions)						Contributions as Percentage of Income Defined as:			Contributions as Percentage of Sales (10)
	Gross Sales (1)	Officers' Compensation (2)	Contributions (3)	Before-Tax Income (4)	After-Tax Income (5)	Dividends (6)	Before-Tax Income (7)	Officers' Compensation, Contributions, and Dividends Paid Out (8)	Officers' Compensation, Contributions, Dividends and Retained Income (9)	
Under $.025	$ 4,999	$ 713	$ 1.17	$ −139	$ −179	$ 58	—	0.15	0.22	0.02
$.025 to .050	8,195	775	1.49	34	−41	28	4.38	0.19	0.20	0.02
.050 to .100	18,082	1,261	4.61	337	149	68	1.37	0.35	0.33	0.03
.100 to .250	44,759	2,186	14.87	1,072	579	182	1.39	0.62	0.53	0.03
.250 to .500	43,961	1,584	19.13	1,212	649	193	1.58	1.07	0.85	0.04
.500 to 1.00	42,171	1,220	25.39	1,386	690	248	1.83	1.70	1.31	0.06
1.00 to 2.50	49,844	1,141	36.49	2,179	1,059	438	1.66	2.26	1.63	0.07
2.50 to 5.00	33,365	636	28.85	1,939	988	419	1.49	2.66	1.75	0.09
5.00 to 10.00	30,778	493	30.56	2,056	1,004	479	1.49	3.05	2.00	0.10
10.00 to 25.00	40,320	493	44.28	3,516	1,842	950	1.26	2.98	1.86	0.11
25.00 to 50.00	26,247	282	28.51	2,485	1,310	726	1.15	2.75	1.76	0.11
50.00 to 100.00	35,345	218	29.89	3,131	1,696	1,155	0.95	2.13	1.54	0.09
100.00 to 250.00	46,812	249	36.36	4,878	2,617	1,875	0.75	1.68	1.25	0.08
250.00 and over	138,383	420	113.48	20,808	12,084	7,982	0.55	1.33	0.90	0.08

SOURCE: U.S. Internal Revenue Service, *Statistics of Income, 1957–8, Corporation Income Tax Returns* (Washington, D.C., 1960), Table 4, pp.39–40.

about the attitudes toward giving expressed by the leaders of large corporations, some of whom were cited above. Certainly, it runs contrary to the widely held belief that the large corporations have been in the vanguard of the liberalization in corporate thinking and behavior in giving. For these reasons and others, the statistical bases of these comparisons were examined in some detail.

One source of bias in the comparison is that the understatement of corporate income may be systematically greater the smaller the company. This bias in income data has been treated more fully elsewhere.[26] In brief, it arises from the inclusion of a return on invested capital in the compensation of the corporation's officers and executives, as well as the salary received for services. The smaller the corporation, the more common it is for its officers to own all or most of the company's stock, and the greater the latitude of these officers in deciding the form of their own compensation. Where both corporate and individual income taxes are involved, there may be significant tax savings if earnings on capital are in the form of salary rather than dividends.

To illustrate the effect of this bias, contributions have been expressed as a percentage of corporate income more broadly defined. Variously included in the two new definitions here presented are officers compensation, and other income components such as dividend payments, retained earnings, and contributions (*Table 15, Columns 8 and 9*). On both definitions of income, the percentage of contributions shows a sharply different relationship to size of company from the one reported above. Corporations in the lowest asset size classes show extremely low giving rates, and the rate is generally higher for the larger corporations than for the smaller. It rises progressively from the smallest size classes to the $5- to $50-million asset range, and then falls off somewhat for the largest asset size classes.

Another kind of bias could arise from the fact that smaller corporations typically might employ relatively more labor than large ones. Corporate profits, which mainly represent payment for the services of capital, might thus represent a smaller part of total factor payments for small than for large corporations. If giving is based on total factor payments or on the total activity of the corporation, it would be a higher percentage of income (the payment to capital) for small corporations. If one were to express the contributions of corporations

---

[26] Joseph L. McConnell, "Corporate Earnings By Size of Firm," *Survey of Current Business*, Washington: U.S. Department of Commerce, May, 1945, pp. 6–12.

as a percentage of their payments to all factors of production (not just to capital), then one might observe a different relationship between giving rate and size.

The evidence suggests that there indeed may be a different relationship. Giving measured against *total* corporate activity rises as corporate size increases. Taking a corporation's gross sales as the measure of its total activity, Column 10 of Table 15 shows that contributions as a percentage of gross sales are generally higher for larger corporations than for smaller.[27] The giving rate, thus measured, rises regularly from the smallest corporations to those in the $10- to $50-million asset range and then falls off a little for those having more than $50 million in assets. Using sales as the measure of size, one could say that, as a general rule, the larger the corporation, the more "generous" it is.

The multiple correlation analysis provides another means for identifying the relationship of size to giving. To answer the question whether the giving percentage is higher for large than for small corporations, we shall seek to determine the scale elasticity of corporate giving. If an elasticity of less than 1 is found, then, other things being equal, a 10 per cent increase in size would mean a less than 10 per cent increase in giving and could be interpreted as evidence that large corporations give proportionately less than small ones. On the other hand, if an elasticity of more than 1 is found, this could be interpreted as evidence that large corporations give proportionately more than small ones.

As in the time-series analysis, the scale variable used in the regressions is income. However, the scale effect represents the relationship between giving and corporate size, assuming that other factors, particularly the rate of return on investment, are held constant. In this analysis, therefore, the scale effect is measured by assuming equiproportionate changes in income and investment, investment here measured by net worth. Thus the scale elasticity is measured as the sum of the income and net-worth coefficients, holding the number of corporations constant. In equations C and D of Table 14, the elasticity is 0.6 to 0.7.

The reasons this may be an understatement were given earlier;

---

[27] A stronger case might be made for measuring contributions relative to value added rather than sales, since value added is a more direct measure of a corporation's separate contribution to economic output. Unfortunately the Internal Revenue Service data are not classified in ways which permit the computa-tion of value-added measures.

namely, the income variable is affected by the composition of officers' compensation, which varies with the size of the corporation. Since the average size of corporations varied widely among the industries used in the cross-sectional analysis, some allowance was made for this effect by including data on officers compensation in the correlation as a separate variable. On a simple correlation basis, as shown in Appendix D, it was positively correlated with each of the other variables in the analysis, and so its influence would be indirectly reflected in the regression coefficients of other variables.

In the multiple regression equations E and F, the beta coefficients of the officers' compensation variable were negative. This deserves some explanation. The figures in Table 15 suggest that the component of officers' compensation representing return on capital, rather than payment for labor services, declined rather sharply as corporate size increased. The table also suggests that, as one rises through successively larger corporate size classes, the pure salary component of officers' compensation probably increases somewhat less than in proportion to corporate size. Presumably the level of compensation for individual officers is subject to greater limitations than the size to which companies can grow. Multiple regression techniques were used to take into account these biases in the gross measure of officers' compensation and so provide a better measure of the effects of size, income, and other factors. The negative beta coefficient suggests that the regression techniques accomplished what they were intended to do.

Were it possible to measure the pure salary part of officers compensation, it could show a negative relationship to giving in the multiple equations, other variables held constant. Officers compensation is a deduction from income, and the higher its value, for corporations of the same size, the lower the corporation's income. Assuming equiproportionate changes in income, net worth, and officers' compensation, the officers' compensation element would represent a negative component in measuring the scale effect. It is not likely, however, that this negative regression coefficient would be very large.

If it were possible to separate out the return-to-capital component of the officers' compensation data, and to assign it to the income variable, the new income variable thus created would vary much less than the one used in the analysis. The regression coefficient for the new income variable would therefore be higher. The combined income and net-worth (i.e. scale) elasticity in equation E of Table 14 is

+.784. Moreover, the size of the officers compensation coefficient ($-.591$) suggests that its effect in overstating the variability in income has been considerable. What the measured scale effect would be, had it been possible to use a more precise measure of income, is difficult to assess. However, when allowance is made for the biases described above, the inference of a scale elasticity not far from $+1$ appears to be reasonable. If so, then it is in rough agreement with that found in the time-series analysis. That is, both findings suggest that larger corporations are neither more nor less generous, relative to their income, than are smaller ones.

Profitability and Giving

One might expect that, in their allocation of funds to contributions, corporate officials would pay particular attention to the profits performance of the company, i.e., how much the company was earning on the investment of its shareholders. The directors of a company with a high return on investment might feel at greater liberty to distribute some profits to charitable causes than those in a company with a low return on investment. This is so because the high-profit company has relatively more resources available for all kinds of spending, including philanthropic contributions. Higher contributions might thus be acceptable to shareholders who, at the same time, may be receiving higher dividends and observing a higher reinvestment of earnings, with its consequences of rapid growth in the value of their investment.

The correlation analysis of the relationship between giving and profits presented above covered the four-year period 1954–1957. This time period was chosen partly because it bears a reasonable operational connection to the experience of corporations. In the long run, rates of return on investment would tend to equality in an economy with high capital mobility, assuming no systematic relationship between long-run risk differences and giving. However, in a period of less than five years, a measurable variation in profit rates among companies might be expected. Such variation could be used in explaining the giving performance of companies.

The coefficients of the profits variable (X_3) can be interpreted as a measure of the responsiveness of giving to the *rate* of profit, i.e., the profitability of corporations. Profitability is measured as the rate of return on invested capital; in this analysis it is the ratio of net profits to net worth (X_4). Because one of the variables included in the estimating equation is net worth, the coefficient of the profits variable reflects the change in giving when all other variables, net worth included, are held constant. Thus a 10 per cent increase in profits, holding net worth constant, signifies a 10 per cent increase in profits as a percentage of net worth.

The responsiveness (elasticity) of giving to profitability, as estimated by the multiple equations excluding the last equation, ranges between .42 and .52. This is roughly in accord with the low-profitability elasticities suggested in the time-series analysis. As pointed out in that examination, corporations might regard high- or low-profit rates as essentially short-run departures from normal rates, and giving might be related more to long-run than to short-run profitability.

While the four-year period covered in the cross-sectional data is long enough to encompass a business cycle (and thus long enough to eliminate some of the distortion that might be found in annual data), it is still a relatively short period—short enough to discourage either low-profit or high-profit firms from basing their giving decisions exclusively on the profit patterns observed in the period.

Employment and Giving

The number of persons engaged by a corporation may be an important factor in the determination of the amount it decides to give. The more employees a corporation has, the more it may feel some responsibility for the welfare of the communities in which they reside. That this has explicit recognition has been demonstrated by surveys of corporation giving.[28] Contributions to local community chest and hospital drives are often based, in important part, on the percentage a company's employees represent in total community employment. Many corporations have college scholarship programs for employees' children, and, in a fairly recent development, some corporations have programs whereby the corporation matches employee alumni gifts to colleges. The changing patterns of contributions described in Chapter Two probably reflect the development of employee-related programs to a considerable degree, particularly in the field of corporate support of higher education.

The hypothesis that a corporation's giving rates are positively re-

---

[28] See, e.g., Andrews, *Corporation Giving*, pp. 47–48, 84–85, and 114–115.

lated to the number of its employees was tested by including data on employment in manufacturing industries (for 1954) in the multiple correlation analysis.[29]

If there were no relationship between number of employees and giving, the coefficient of the employment variable (X_5) should be zero. If, on the other hand, the number of employees were the sole determinant of the amount given, then one might infer that the co-efficient of X_5 would be 1. That is, if a corporation's giving were rigidly based on a fixed number of dollars per employee, one would observe giving to rise in direct proportion to employment.

The observed coefficient of the employment variable is positive and significantly greater than zero (+.270). This value predicts that a corporation with 10 per cent more employees than another having the same dimensions in all other respects (size, profits, officers' compensation) will give 2.7 per cent more in contributions. The coefficient thus provides some notion of the importance of the number of employees in a corporation's giving. Accounting for a 27-per-cent part of what would be a fully proportionate response, it must be numbered among the more important factors determining a corporation's giving level.

Dividends and Giving

The contributions of a corporation represent a distribution of its earnings to persons and institutions other than its shareholders. The benefits to the company and its shareholders of these gifts is often indirect and possibly long deferred. Therefore, in the context of immediate and measurable gain, a company's contributions are a subtraction from the shareholders' claim on its earnings. This, of course, is not always so. In many cases, the gain to the company and ultimately to the shareholders far outweighs the cost of the gift. For example, corporate support of hospitals in communities in which a large pro-

---

[29] Industry employment data came from the Bureau of the Census, whereas data on corporate profits, net worth, contributions, etc. came from the Internal Revenue Service. The two sets of data are not wholly comparable, as the Census data are based on the manufacturing *establishments* classified in the given industry group, while the Internal Revenue Service data are based on *companies*. Where a company has a number of establishments, some falling in one industry group and some in others, the Internal Revenue Service assigns it to the industry group of greatest activity. Neither the degree nor the direction of the bias introduced into the present analysis from this source is known. However, it is likely to be small, as the industry groups are quite broad, and the number of companies having operations in more than one group—operations which account for a significant part of the activities of each of the several groups—is likely to be few.

portion of residents work in the company's plant may so reduce costs of labor absenteeism, for health reasons, as to more than repay the cost of supporting the hospital. And, indeed, much of the judicial support of the legality of corporate giving is based on the argument that the corporation does in some sense realize some value from the gifts it makes, and this undoubtedly has much influence on corporate giving policies.

In addition, the extent to which contributions reduce dividends may be operationally insignificant. Contributions represent only a minor fraction of corporate earnings distributions—for all corporations less than 3 per cent of dividends and contributions combined (*Table 16, column 4*). The percentage varies considerably among the major industrial sectors, but in no sector is it more than 11 per cent. Moreover, some of the larger percentages may reflect the inadequacy of the dividend data in describing the distribution of earnings. The sectors having the three largest percentages are construction, trade, and services, in which the average corporation size is small. As was shown earlier, smaller companies more commonly tend to distribute earnings as part of officers compensation and place less emphasis on dividend distributions. To the degree that officers compensation represents a distribution of profit rather than a pure payment for services, gifts as a per cent of gifts plus dividends overstates the importance of gifts in total distributions of earnings.

To demonstrate this bias, gifts have been expressed as a percentage of the total of dividends, officers compensation, and gifts (*Table 16, column 5*). This of course is an overadjustment, as much of the officers compensation is true payment for services. However, there was no feasible way of separating out the "dividend component" of officers compensation. Even though the percentage of gifts to total distributions of earnings is now understated, the percentages for the various industrial sectors are more comparable. The percentages for construction, trade, and services are now the same general size as the other groups, and the relative variation among sectors is much lower. On the broader definition, therefore, the substitution of contributions for dividends is on the order of about 2 per cent of dividends.

In the multiple correlation analysis presented in Table 14, an attempt was made to directly determine the effect on contributions of dividend payments. This was done by including dividends as one of the explanatory variables (*Equation F*). The appearance of the dividends resulted in sharp changes in the estimating coefficients for the

TABLE 16   Gifts and Contributions as Percentage of Total Distributions of Corporation Earnings, All Corporations and Eight Major Industrial Sectors, 1954–1955 through 1957–1958
(Dollar values in millions)

| Industrial Sector | Annual Averages of | | | Contributions as a Percentage of Distributions | |
| | | | | Distributions Measured as: | |
	Dividends Other Than Own Stock (1)	Officers' Compensation (2)	Gifts and Contributions (3)	Contributions and Dividends (4)	Contributions, Officers' Compensation and Dividends (5)
All corporations	$13,615	$10,459	$388	2.77	1.59
Agriculture, forestry and fisheries	47	90	1	2.50	0.87
Mining and quarrying	761	124	7	0.85	0.73
Construction	84	668	10	10.68	1.31
Manufacturing	6,769	3,475	220	3.14	2.10
Public utilities	2,413	4,061	29	1.14	0.98
Trade	999	3,054	66	6.21	1.61
Finance, insurance, and real estate	2,364	1,451	45	1.87	1.17
Services	177	721	11	6.02	1.25

SOURCE: *Statistics of Income, 1954, 1955, 1956–7, 1957–8*, pp. 44–51, 31–38, 25–32, 31–38 respectively.

profits and net worth variables, and noticeable changes in the other variables. Whereas the coefficients of equations having successively more variables up to this point had appeared to evolve in a rather orderly manner, the introduction of dividends drastically reordered the estimating equation. The observed estimating coefficient of the dividend variable was very high ($+.709$).

Two interpretations of this pattern present themselves. The first is that the influence of dividends is clearly of a lower order of magnitude than scale of operations and profitability. If so, then the observed change assigning more influence to dividends is primarily statistical. The intercorrelations between dividends and income (scale) is high ($+.871$), as is that between dividends and net worth ($+.885$). When dividends were added to the equation it was therefore the idiosyncrasies of multicollinearity, rather than the discovery of a significant new explanatory variable, that produced the change.

The second interpretation is that, considered in their short-run operational context, the dividend and contributions decisions are likely to produce parallel short-run changes in these two distributions of corporate income. Corporate managements may be reluctant to increase contributions if, at the same time, they decide not to increase dividends. While it is true that contributions amount to only 2 or 3 per cent of dividends, management may fear some loss of stockholder good will if it became known that contributions were increased while dividends were not. Although both distributions are primarily determined by longer-run factors, in a cross-sectional, short-run comparison, the parallel movements in the two, for the reasons cited above, might assign to dividends a more pervasive causal significance than they actually have.

The qualitative evidence on this issue is mixed. In his survey of shareholder attempts to limit contributions by corporations, John H. Watson III found that

> The vast majority of stockholders approve the practice—at least by default—since relatively few either endorse or complain about management's decision. But those who do complain are usually aggressive in stating their disapproval. They demand and get management attention. . . . On balance, however, the playback from stockholders praises company contributions.

Watson qualifies his review, however, in the following way:

> But despite the present success of corporate management in administering the company's contribution policy to the satisfaction of all but

a minority of its stockholders, every management acknowledges it must be cautious in exercising control. For no one responding to the NICB survey ruled out the possibility that less prosperous times might bring challenges from more formidable stockholders.[30]

SUMMARY

The effects of the scale of corporate operations could be measured using both time-series and cross-sectional data. Both analyses estimated a scale elasticity of close to +1. This suggests that, by virtue of size alone, large corporations give neither more, nor less, in proportion to their size than do small ones.

The correlation analyses based on time-series data suggested that the price elasticity of giving had a value of close to −1. Price was here measured as the complement of the marginal tax rate, and so represented the after-tax cost of $1 in giving. The observed elasticity suggested that the immediate and certain tax reduction that results from contributions was a significant factor in the giving decision. This was plausible, particularly when the assessment of the other benefits from contributions must necessarily be very uncertain.

The analysis assigned considerable significance to the growth in corporate giving propensity, i.e., to an increased and more widespread acceptance of its legality, appropriateness, and worth. After taking separate account of price and scale effects, progressive changes in the effects of other factors, of which the change in giving propensity was judged to be the most important, were found to be very significant. Changes in other factors, thus measured, accounted for a more than 300 per cent increase in gifts and contributions (constant dollars) over the twenty-seven-year period 1936–1963.

Both the time-series and the cross-sectional analyses suggested a rather low degree of responsiveness of giving to changes in the rate of return on shareholders investment (profitability). The finding seemed plausible. Corporations might regard periods of high or low profit rates as temporary, and might, therefore, relate giving to their longer-run profit rates. Probably more important in the immediate operational context, giving might be most directly related to the absolute amount of income as, for example, it is under the tax regulations. If so, considerations of rate of return are a step removed from the central decision variables.

---

[30] "Corporate Contributions Policy," *The Conference Board Record*, National Industrial Conference Board, June, 1967, pp. 12–14.

The relationship between giving and employment was measured, using cross-sectional data. The correlation analysis found a significant association between the relative degree to which corporations used labor in production and the level of giving. Prior examination of giving patterns had found much of corporate giving to be employee-related. Contributions to community fund drives are frequently based on quotas determined by the number of the company's employees in the community. More recently, educational grants for employees and their children have received increased emphasis.

Finally, the cross-sectional analysis brought out a significant association between contributions and dividend payments. Probably both forms of corporate income distribution reflect a common cause, namely the income (or scale of activity) on which they are both based. However, the degree of the association suggests a possibly significant degree of short-run interrelationship. Possibly corporate management would not feel justified in increasing contributions with no concurrent increase in dividends. This, despite the fact that contributions represent only 2 or 3 per cent of dividend payments.

FOUR
⚓⚓⚓

Company-Sponsored
Foundations

IN RECENT years, particularly since 1950, many corporations have channeled their contributions through philanthropic foundations. It is the purpose of this chapter to measure the importance of company-sponsored foundations in total corporate giving, and to determine the degree to which the use of these foundations may have altered the patterns previously observed in the tax return data.

Tax return data on contributions are not classified by type of recipient, and so there is no way to measure precisely the amount channeled through company-sponsored foundations, or of identifying its growth over the period. Other data, available only since 1956, indicate that about one-fourth of total corporate contributions was channeled through company-sponsored foundations (*Table 17*). This share has apparently held fairly constant through the 1956–1965 decade, though the data are probably too rough to distinguish trends.

As mentioned above, there is no direct way of describing the growth to this level from earlier years. Viewed from the foundation's side, probably most of the growth took place in the early 1950's, with earlier and smaller growth occurring during World War II. In a tabulation of 1,472 of the largest company-sponsored foundations of 1965, 1,150, or 78 per cent, were founded in 1950 or later.[1] Of these, 620 were established in the four Korean War excess-profits tax years, 1950–1953, and 283 in 1954–1957. The four World War II years, 1942–1945, saw a minor peak, 172 foundations being organized in that period. Of the $1.3 billion in 1963 assets held by the 1,472 foundations, 60 per cent was held by foundations organized in 1950–

---

[1] Marianna O. Lewis, Editor, *The Foundation Directory, Edition 3* (New York: Russell Sage Foundation, 1967), p. 29.

TABLE 17   The Percentage of Corporate Contributions Channeled Through Company-Sponsored Foundations, 1956–1958, 1960–1962, and 1964–1965 (Dollar values in millions)

Period	Average Annual Contributions Reported on Tax Returns All Corporations (1)	Average Annual Expenditures Tabulated Foundations (2)	Number in Tabulation (3)	Column (2) as Percentage of Column (1) (4)
1956–1958	$410	$108	1,320	26.3
1960–1962	530	149	1,716	28.1
1964–1965	752	181	1,472	24.1

sources: *Column (1): 1956–58, 1960–62, 1964*, Appendix Table I; *1965*, extrapolation of 1964 value of $729 million, based on the compound annual growth rate of 6.4 per cent found for the growth from 1955 through 1964. *Columns (2) and (3): 1956–58*, Ann D. Walton and F. Emerson Andrews, Editors, *The Foundation Directory, Edition 1* (New York: Russell Sage Foundation, 1960), Table 6, p. xxii; *1960–62*, Ann D. Walton and Marianna O. Lewis, Editors, *The Foundation Directory, Edition 2* (New York: Russell Sage Foundation, 1964), Table 9, p. 30; *1964–65*, Marianna O. Lewis, Editor, *The Foundation Directory, Edition 3* (New York: Russell Sage Foundation, 1967), Table 13, pp. 32–33. It should be noted that, in Editions 1 and 2, a company-sponsored foundation was defined as one which had a corporation or partnership as a direct contributor. This definition was tightened, in Edition 3, from "direct contributor" to "principal contributor," with resulting reductions in expenditures and members. The amount of this reduction is not known, but probably not substantial.

1957 and 9 per cent by those organized since 1957. Only 20 per cent was held by foundations organized before 1946.

THE FUNCTIONS OF COMPANY-SPONSORED FOUNDATIONS

Company-sponsored foundations are nonprofit corporations or trusts whose stated purpose is the support of cultural, scientific, and educational activities. They enjoy tax-exempt status, and contributions to them are tax deductible from the income of the sponsoring corporations. The foundations, in turn, distribute these funds to charitable beneficiaries. The foundations' policies are controlled by boards of trustees, who are usually officers and directors of the sponsoring corporations.

As financial intermediaries between donor corporations and charitable recipients, company-sponsored foundations may serve several functions. One is to smooth the flow of corporate giving. Corporation profits are subject to wide fluctuations and, were giving tied too closely to them, corporate giving programs also would be unstable. Instability, it is commonly believed, serves to weaken the effects of giving programs, where sustained and regular support of philanthropic activities is desired.

Company-sponsored foundations also permit corporations to exercise discretion in the timing of their contributions. In low-profit years, corporations may be under pressure to trim all nonessential and deferrable outlays, and giving may be prominent among these. Conversely, in years of high profits, management may find it advantageous to increase the percentage of income given. The after-tax cost of giving might not only be lower, but the higher level of contributions produces a more stable income record for public presentation. Company-sponsored foundations, as reservoirs to be filled in good years and drained in lean years, permit such discretionary spacing of a company's contributions.

Foundations also may accumulate funds. Corporations, for a period of time, may make transfers to their foundations well in excess of the foundations' charitable outlays, thus building up endowment funds. The foundations may then use the income from their capital to support their grant programs. Though not common, some corporations have built the endowment of their foundations to the point that investment earnings support the major part of their spending programs. Such corporations, of course, enjoy even greater freedom in the timing of future grants to their foundations.

As will be shown below, an important factor in the timing of large endowment grants to company-sponsored foundations has been the episodic appearance of the excess-profits tax. In years of high excess-profits tax rates, transfers to company-sponsored foundations can be made at a low net cost to the donor corporations. The income from the capital thus transferred can then be used to support the foundations' program outlays, replacing part of the corporations' regular contributions to their foundations. Corporations, in effect, can maintain part of their philanthropic programs on the lower net-cost basis prevailing at the time of the excess-profits tax.[2]

The building of endowment funds makes the flow of corporate contributions that move through company-sponsored foundations a complex one. In the mid-1960's, for example, the 1,472 foundations held assets aggregating $1,307 million. They received annual gifts totaling $206 million and made annual outlays of $181 million. If one as-

---

[2] For a more extensive discussion of the advantages and disadvantages of the company-sponsored foundations, see: John H. Watson III, *Company-Sponsored Foundations*, Studies in Business Policy, No. 73 (New York: National Industrial Conference Board, 1955); Frank M. Andrews, *A Study of Company-Sponsored Foundations* (New York: Russell Sage Foundation, 1960); F. Emerson Andrews, *Corporation Giving* (New York: Russell Sage Foundation, 1952).

sumes that they earned 4 per cent on their assets, their investment income for the year would have been $52 million. Against receipts of contributions and income of $258 million, expenditures were $181 million (of which outright grants were $177 million); capital thus would be increased by $77 million per year.[3]

GROWTH OF ENDOWMENT SINCE 1950

To provide a more precise picture of the effect of the growth of endowments on contribution flows, the record for a group of the largest company-sponsored foundations was examined in some detail.[4] Balance sheet data for 169 foundations were available for 1951, 1956, and 1960, and aggregate income and expenditures data were used for the ten-year period 1951–1960.[5]

While not permitting an examination of year-to-year changes, these data made it possible to isolate the period of greatest endowment (in the early 1950's) from the late 1950's, when grants for capital purposes were less important. Data on investment income, contributions received, and philanthropic expenditures later became available for the early 1960's, for 170 foundations.[6] Of these, 162 were the same as those on the 1951–1960 list.[7]

---

[3] Foundations sponsored by family-owned corporations receive gifts not only from the corporation, most often for current disbursements, but also from the individuals and families involved. A considerable part of the $1,307 million in assets represents endowment gifts from such individuals and families. The estimated growth in assets thus may be as much the result of personal as it is of "purely corporate" contributions. (*See note 17, below*.)

[4] This examination of fund flows draws heavily on material presented in Ralph L. Nelson, *The Investment Policies of Foundations* (New York: Russell Sage Foundation, 1967), Chapter 5. There, the record for the period 1951–1960 was presented. Here, the record has been updated through 1964.

[5] The 169 foundations here examined were taken from the 534 for which Representative Wright Patman presented 1951–1960 data in *Tax Exempt Foundations and Charitable Trusts—Their Impact on Our Economy*, Chairman's Report to the Select Committee on Small Business, House of Representatives, 87th Congress, December 31, 1962. Of the 534 in the Patman Report, 177 were among those classified by F. Emerson Andrews as company-sponsored in worksheets for his statistical introduction to *The Foundation Directory, Edition 1*, edited by Ann D. Walton and F. Emerson Andrews (New York: Russell Sage Foundation, 1960). The Patman tables provided balance sheets only for 1951 (or beginning-year balance sheets if organized after 1951) and 1960. A comparison of endowment growth between the earlier and later parts of the decade was made from 1956 Internal Revenue returns for 169 of the 177 foundations. The 1956 data were obtained from the files of the Foundation Library Center.

[6] *Tax Exempt Foundations and Charitable Trusts—Their Impact on our Economy*, Fourth Installment, Subcommittee Chairman's Report to Subcommittee No. 1, Select Committee on Small Business, House of Representatives, 89th Congress, December 21, 1966, pp. 15–56.

[7] The eight new ones and seven displaced ones were, on average, relatively small foundations.

TABLE 18   Growth in Total Assets of 169 Company-Sponsored
Foundations, 1951–1956, 1956–1960
(Dollar values in millions)

Year	*169 Foundations*
Total assets:	
(1) 1951 or first year thereafter	$138.5
(2) 1956	389.5
(3) 1960	434.8
Change in assets between:	
(4) 1951, or first year thereafter, and 1956	251.0
(5) 1956 and 1960	45.3
(6) First balance-sheet assets of foundations organized in 1951 through 1953	45.2
Total 1951–1960:	
(7) Increase in assets (4) + (5) + (6)	341.5
(8) Increase in liabilities	13.2
(9) Increase in net worth (7) − (8)	$328.3

SOURCE: Ralph L. Nelson, *The Investment Policies of Foundations* (New York: Russell Sage Foundation, 1967), Table 22, p. 129.

1951–1956

The asset growth of the 169 foundations, from 1951 to 1960, is described in Table 18. Ninety-one of these foundations were organized from 1951 through 1953, years in which the excess-profits tax was in effect. The first balance sheets for the 91 reported assets totaling $45.2 million. Presumably these represented, in the main, initial gifts from the sponsoring corporation. Although expenditures data for the first year of operation are not available, the total for the longer period and allowance for an upward trend suggest that they were probably no more than $20 million, leaving $25–$30 million of the total as initial endowment grants.

By the end of 1956, the 169 foundations saw their assets grow by $251 million.[8] Since the excess-profits tax was removed in 1954, it is possible that the endowment-building gifts of the sponsoring corpora-

---

[8] The growth in assets is based on the ledger or book values, not market value. This is, of course, the appropriate way of treating them for present purposes. Ledger value represents the value at which the corporation transferred assets to its foundation, and as such provides a more precise description of the endowing process. Ledger value also reflects capital gains realized by the foundation on the sale of its assets, and this, to some degree, distorts the picture. The distortion is not large, however. In 1960, the 169 foundations had a combined ledger value of $434.8 million, and realized capital gains for the period 1951–1960 of only $3.9 million. The 1960 market value was $566.5 million.

tions were made in 1954, 1955, or 1956, and not in response to excess-profits tax considerations. Although the annual data that could answer this question are not available, a review of the time pattern of total corporate giving suggests that 1954–1956 were not endowment-building years. A straight-line growth trend connecting 1949 to 1959 places contributions for the three years 1951–1953 at an average of $111 million per year above the trend. Those for the three years 1954–1956 average only $3 million per year above the trend. It is reasonable to assume that corporations projected relatively regular increases in distributions to philanthropic agencies over the period, and so the "surplus above trend" can be taken as providing a rough measure of contributions used principally to build endowment.

1956–1960

The period from 1956 to 1960 was one of normal corporate income tax rates. Accordingly, the period could be expected to exhibit a more "normal" pattern of fund flows through company-sponsored foundations. In this period the total assets of the 169 foundations grew by $45.3 million. By comparison, the initial endowment and subsequent asset growth of the same foundations in the early 1950's was six times as large. The 1956–1960 growth suggests that the building of endowment was not exclusively associated with the excess-profits tax. Corporations found it appropriate to continue to give liberally not only to sustain their foundations' giving programs, but also to continue to build endowment.

The continuing process of endowment building is reflected in the experience of individual foundations (*Table 19*). From the early 1950's to 1956, 156 of the 169 foundations experienced an increase in assets, and only 10 a decrease. Growth in assets was almost universal. From 1956 to 1960 a smaller number (105) showed an in-

TABLE 19   Change in Asset Size, 169 of Largest Company-Sponsored Foundations, Early 1950's to 1956 and 1956 to 1960

	Number of Foundations	
Direction of Change	*Early 1950's–1956*	*1956–1960*
Decrease	10	63
No change	3	1
Increase	156	105
	169	169

SOURCE: Based on Ralph L. Nelson, *The Investment Policies of Foundations* (New York: Russell Sage Foundation, 1967), Table 23, p. 132.

crease, but this was two-thirds again the number that showed a decrease (63). Though less universal, growth in assets was still by far the more common experience.[9]

1961–1964

As indicated above, the absence of balance-sheet data precludes direct measurement of the growth in asset values for 1961 through 1964. However, data on receipts and expenditures for 170 foundations permit an indirect calculation of this growth.[10] The calculations are presented in columns 1 through 5 of Table 20. They show that assets grew by about $53 million, or by somewhat more than their growth in the preceding four-year period.

The table shows also that the foundations' expenditures on grants continued to grow over the four-year period, rising from $63 million in 1961 to $82 million in 1964. In the early 1960's, as in the late 1950's, foundations appear to have expanded their giving programs while at the same time adding to their endowments. Investment income seems to have been used to support grants in excess of receipts from sponsoring corporations and to build endowment, with about one-half being devoted to each purpose.

The pattern was not uniform over time, however. Although contributions to philanthropy by the 170 foundations showed an unbroken and fairly steady year-to-year growth, the pattern of asset growth reflected fluctuations in contributions from donor corporations, which showed a dip from 1962 to 1963, followed by a sharp rise from 1963 to 1964.

EFFECT ON THE FLOW OF TOTAL COPORATE CONTRIBUTIONS

The above findings suggest that the use by corporations of company-sponsored foundations has had a measurable and significant effect on the flow of contributions from donor corporations to the ultimate recipients. It is the purpose of this section to generalize the findings from the group of examined foundations, and so to gauge the effect of

---

[9] The relation between endowment status and the investment policies of company-sponsored foundations is explored in greater detail in Nelson, *op. cit.*, Chapter 5.

[10] The basic list of company-sponsored foundations was 177, as indicated in note 4 above. For the 1951–1960 period, only 169 were examined, owing to the absence of 1956 balance-sheet data for 8. The 170 on the 1961–1964 list include 41 of the largest foundations in the group of 177. Size is measured by 1960 expenditures, the 42 largest each having made expenditures of at least $300,000 in that year. The 170, as a group, accounted for 95.8 per cent of total 1951–1960 expenditures of $430.7 million for all 177.

TABLE 20   Receipts and Expenditures of 170 Large Company-Sponsored
Foundations, 1961–1964 Compared to 1951–1960
(In millions of dollars)

	1964 (1)	1963 (2)	1962 (3)	1961 (4)	1961–64 (5)	1951–60 (6)
Receipts						
Gifts from donor corporations and others	$ 73.8	$58.4	$61.5	$54.1	$247.8	$587.9
Investment income	26.2	25.1	24.1	24.9	100.4	142.2
Total receipts	$100.0	$83.5	$85.6	$79.0	$348.2	$730.1
Expenditures on grants program and administration	82.3	77.7	72.3	63.2	295.5	412.5
Indicated increase in assets	$ 17.7	$ 5.8	$13.3	$15.8	$ 52.7	$317.6ᵃ

ᵃ The indicated increase in assets for all the foundations in the basic list was $318 million. This compares with an increase of $356 million derived by comparing beginning- and ending-year balance sheets. Balance-sheet totals of $328 million for 169 of the 177 foundations are presented in Table 18, above. The 8 other foundations recorded a balance sheet of $28 million. This $38-million discrepancy between estimated ($318) and direct ($356) asset change data reflects several things. The largest is $22 million in real- ized capital gains that are reflected in increased asset values on balance sheets, but which are not included in the data on receipts and expenditures in this table. Another source of the discrepancy is that book values of assets may reflect revaluations which were not car- ried over into income statements. This was a period of rising security prices, and pre- sumably most revaluations were upward. In the case of one foundation, there apparently was a jump in size resulting from the acquisition of another foundation, the latter being that of the company the sponsoring corporation had acquired through merger. Here, assets would have increased without corresponding entries on the income statement. Finally, it appeared that, in a few cases, asset increases reflected either gifts or capital gains not reported on the foundations' financial statements. Examinations of individual foundations indicated that such differences were typically small enough to allow one to infer that the fund-flow magnitudes here described are reasonably accurate.

company-sponsored foundations on total corporate giving.[11] It will be convenient to distinguish two stages in the process, the endowing and the endowed stage. During the endowing stage, recipient charities will receive less than the amount given by the corporation, the balance being used to expand the foundation's assets. In the endowed stage, recipients may receive more than the corporation gives, the difference being covered by earnings on endowment and possibly also by a draw- ing down of capital. This section seeks to estimate the magnitude of these differences.

---

[11] The foundations in the list were selected not by the size of their assets but rather by the size of their expenditures. They are considered more representative of company-sponsored foundations in general than a selection based on assets, since the latter principle of selection would have been biased in favor of those foundations emphasizing the build-up of endowment.

TABLE 21 Estimated Flow of Corporate Contributions, 1951–1956, 1957–1960, and 1961–1964 (Dollar values in millions)

	1951–56	*1957–60*	*1961–64*
Sources of Philanthropic Funds			
(1) Contributions from corporations reported on tax returns	$2,384	$1,776	$2,460
(2) Investment earnings of company-sponsored foundations	145	115	170
TOTAL	$2,529	$1,891	$2,630
Disposition of Funds			
(3) Increase endowment of company-sponsored foundations	400	65	90
(4) Distributions to philanthropic beneficiaries	2,129	1,826	2,540
TOTAL	$2,529	$1,891	$2,630
(5) Line 4 as percentage of Line 1	89.3	102.8	103.3

The six-year period 1951–1956 witnessed the endowing stage in pronounced degree. The growth of all company-sponsored foundations, owing to their receipt of sponsoring corporation gifts, may be estimated at $400 million.[12] Total corporate contributions reported on tax returns were $2,384 million for the six-year period. Income from the accumulating endowments of company-sponsored foundations probably added about $145 million,[13] making total receipts of $2,529 million. Subtracting the $400 million allocated to building of endowments leaves an estimated $2,129 million distributed to charitable activities. In the aggregate, therefore, recipient philanthropic agencies received about eight-ninths of the amount that corporations gave, with one-ninth having been used to increase endowment (*Table 21*). For companies with foundations, of course, the proportion going into endowment was typically much higher than one-ninth.

The four years 1957 through 1960 trace a pattern of fund flows

---

[12] The estimate was made as follows: First, the net assets of the 169 foundations for which data were available increased by $245 million in this period. Making a rough deduction for contributions from individuals and families reduced the growth in net assets to about $200 million. In 1956 the 169 foundations, with assets of $390 million, accounted for 51 per cent of the assets of the 1,320 company-sponsored foundations tabulated in the first edition of *The Foundation Directory*. The growth of all foundations was then taken as twice that of the 169, or about $400 million.

[13] This was estimated using a 4-per-cent rate of return on an average estimated endowment of $600 million for six years.

more characteristic of the endowed stage. The asset growth of all foundations, reflecting sponsoring corporation gifts, is estimated at $65 million. Corporation contributions reported on tax returns totaled $1,776 million, with the endowment income of company-sponsored foundations adding $115 million.[14] Of total receipts of $1,891 million, $65 million was allocated to increase the foundations' endowment, leaving $1,826 million to be distributed to philanthropic activities. Thus recipients received roughly 3 per cent more than the corporation gave in the four years.

The four years 1961–1964 also present a pattern of fund flows more typical of the endowed stage. The 1964 expenditures of the 170 foundations totaled $82 million, or about 45 per cent of the $181 million spent by the 1,470-odd company-sponsored foundations tabulated in Edition 3 of *The Foundation Directory.* Allowing for direct contributions to these foundations by individuals and families connected with the sponsoring corporations, the flow of strictly corporate donations through all company-sponsored foundations may be estimated to be one-and-seven-tenths of that for the group of 170.

Based on this extrapolation, the assets of all company-sponsored foundations grew by about $90 million over the four-year period. Endowment earnings totaled about $170 million, implying a net addition of $80 million to total corporate contributions of $2,460 million. Thus charitable recipients received $2,540 million or roughly 3 per cent more than corporations gave in the four-year period. The estimates are too crude to identify small changes, but they suggest that endowment earnings added a slightly higher percentage to the receipts of charitable organizations in the period 1961–1964 than they did in 1956–1960.

In terms of the over-all flow of corporate contributions, the above findings suggest that the endowed and semi-endowed status of some company-sponsored foundations is presently having only a small effect. This derives primarily from two factors. First, endowment income accounts for only 25 to 30 per cent of the total receipts of the foundations,[15] and second, company-sponsored foundations as a group

---

[14] This was estimated using a 4-per-cent rate of return on an average estimated endowment of $720 million for four years. The higher average endowment reflects an estimated $65 million in asset growth from new contributions, and a rise in income from higher dividend payments, here expressed as higher value of endowment.

[15] Nelson, *The Investment Policies of Foundations,* Table 26, p. 137.

TABLE 22 Types of Donors to Company-Sponsored Foundations

	42 Larger Foundations	*135 Smaller Foundations*
Company only	40	102
Companies and individuals	1	21
Individuals only	1	5
No donor indicated	0	7
TOTAL	42	135

SOURCE: Ralph L. Nelson, *The Investment Policies of Foundations* (New York: Russell Sage Foundation, 1967), Table 25, p. 135.

distribute only one-fourth of total corporate contributions.[16] It follows that the findings based on tax return data presented in Chapters Two and Three apply with almost as much validity to the receipts of philanthropic agencies as they do to the philanthropic outlays of corporations. This probably has been true for most of the period from the late 1930's through the early 1960's. The most important departure probably occurred in the early 1950's, when excess-profits-tax inducements led many corporations to allocate a significant part of their abnormally high contributions to the building of their foundations' endowments.

THE MIX OF FAMILY AND CORPORATE SUPPORT OF COMPANY-SPONSORED FOUNDATIONS

Many company-sponsored foundations receive a considerable part of their support directly from individuals and families. The degree of family involvement is usually greater for smaller corporations than for the larger ones. The larger ones are more often widely held enterprises, with many stockholders, and with no single individual or family predominant in its affairs. In smaller corporations, one often finds foundations in a process of transition from conduits for current giving, with little capital, to endowed agencies that have received large blocks of the family's business as part of estate planning or as charitable bequests. In these foundations, the income from investments is likely to support a larger fraction of their philanthropic programs than in the foundations of larger, widely held corporations.

That personal or family interests are more common among smaller foundations is suggested in Table 22, which compares the personal

---

[16] See Table 17, above.

TABLE 23   Level and Growth of Endowment Income Support of Company-Sponsored Foundations' Philanthropic Program, 1951–1960 and 1961–1964
(Dollar values in millions)

1951–1960	42 Larger Foundations	135 Smaller Foundations
(1) Expenditures on program	$261.9	$168.8
(2) Investment income	61.2	91.6
(3) Gifts and contributions received	386.1	209.5
(4) Implied increase in endowment (2) + (3) − (1)	185.5	132.3
(5) Investment income as percentage of expenditures on program (2) as % of (1)	23.4	54.2
(6) Percent of gifts received "allocated" to increase in endowment (4) as % of (3)	48.0	63.1

1961–1964	41 Larger Foundations	129 Smaller Foundations
(7) Expenditures on program	$178.7	$116.7
(8) Investment income	50.1	50.2
(9) Gifts and contributions received	161.0	86.8
(10) Implied increase in endowment (8) + (9) − (7)	32.4	20.3
(11) Investment income as percentage of expenditures on program (2) as % of (1)	28.0	43.0
(12) Percent of gifts received "allocated" to increase in endowment, (10) as % of (9)	20.1	23.4

or business composition of the names of donors for 177 foundations classified as company-sponsored.[17] Relatively more of the 135 smaller foundations had recognizable personal or family donors than the 42 larger ones.

The degree of family involvement also is reflected in the importance of investment income in the support of philanthropic programs. As shown in Table 23, investment earnings supported a higher percent-

---

[17] *The Foundation Directory* and files of the Foundation Library Center were examined to determine whether the names of persons as well as companies appeared among the donors to the foundation. This classification is necessarily rough, since for many foundations the list of donors was probably incomplete. And, of course, the listing of donors by name provides no measure of the amounts contributed by each.

In his classification of foundations for *The Foundation Directory*, Mr. Andrews has indicated that he included as company-sponsored all those in which a company's name appeared among the list of donors. For the many cases in which

age of the philanthropic programs of the smaller than of the larger foundations. In 1951–1960, earnings on endowment supported 54 per cent of the expenditures of the 135 smaller foundations, and only 23 per cent of the expenditures of the 42 larger ones (*row 5*). The difference between the two groups was smaller in 1961–1964, 43 as compared to 28 per cent (*row 11*), suggesting that the larger foundations had become more highly endowed, while the smaller ones had become less highly endowed.

This interpretation may be premature, however. Rows 6 and 12 of Table 23 suggest that, in both 1951–1960 and 1961–1964, the smaller foundations allocated a higher percentage of gifts received to the building of endowment than did the larger ones. Possibly the larger foundations emphasized investments with higher interest and dividend yields than did the smaller ones. In any event, it appears that the large, widely held, corporations have made substantial advances in the endowed status of their foundations.

---

information was sparse or vague, he classified a foundation as company-sponsored if there appeared to be some connection with a business. For example, The Cooper Foundation of Lincoln, Nebraska, was classified as company-sponsored even though Joseph H. Cooper was the only donor listed. This was done in the light of its Statement of Purpose, which read in part: "In general, funds [are] distributed only in areas where the Foundation's theater properties are located (Nebraska, Colorado and Oklahoma)." One might also have classified the Foundation as a personal one, on the theory that Mr. Cooper's theater business was the vehicle used by him to conduct his personal philanthropies. About the only foundations which are clearly just vehicles for corporate giving in its institutional sense are those of the largest corporations whose shareholders are many and dispersed and where management is separated from ownership.

For discussion of another problem of classification, see Nelson, *op. cit.*, Table 22, p. 129.

Appendixes

Appendix A Basic Tables on Gross National Product and Corporate Contributions, Income and Tax Rates, 1936–1964

APPENDIX TABLE I Corporate Contributions as Percentage of Gross National Product

Year	Gross National Product Current Dollars (Billions)	Gross National Product 1936 Dollars (Billions)	Gifts and Contributions (Millions) Current Dollars	Gifts and Contributions (Millions) 1936 Dollars	Gifts and Contributions (Millions) Percentage of GNP	Implicit Price Deflator (1936= 100)
1936	$ 82.5	$ 82.5	$ 30	$ 30.0	.0364	100.0
1937	90.4	86.9	33	31.7	.0365	104.2
1938	84.7	82.5	27	26.3	.0319	102.8
1939	90.5	89.5	31	30.6	.0342	101.2
1940	99.7	97.1	38	37.0	.0381	102.8
1941	124.5	112.7	58	52.48	.0466	110.5
1942	157.9	127.3	98	79.0	.0621	124.1
1943	191.6	144.1	159	119.54	.0830	133.0
1944	210.1	154.4	234	171.7	.1112	136.3
1945	212.0	151.9	266	190.3	.1253	139.8
1946	208.5	133.6	214	137.0	.1025	156.2
1947	231.3	132.5	241	138.0	.1042	174.7
1948	257.6	138.4	239	128.2	.0926	186.4
1949	256.5	138.5	223	120.4	.0869	185.2
1950	284.8	151.9	252	134.2	.0883	187.8
1951	328.4	163.9	343	171.1	.1044	200.5
1952	345.5	168.9	399	194.7	.1153	204.9
1953	364.6	176.5	495	239.4	.1356	206.8
1954	364.8	174.0	314	149.7	.0860	209.8
1955	398.0	187.2	415	194.9	.1041	212.9
1956	419.2	190.7	418	189.9	.0996	220.1
1957	441.1	193.4	417	182.7	.0945	228.3
1958	447.3	191.2	395	168.7	.0882	234.2
1959	483.6	203.3	482	202.6	.0996	237.9
1960	503.8	208.5	482	199.3	.0956	241.9
1961	520.1	212.6	512	209.0	.0983	245.0
1962	560.3	226.6	595	240.4	.1061	247.5
1963	589.2	235.1	657	262.0	.1114	250.8
1964	628.7	246.9	729	285.9	.1160	255.0

SOURCES: *Gross National Product* and *Implicit Price Deflator:* U.S. Department of Commerce, *Survey of Current Business,* August, 1965, pp. 24–25; 52–53. *Corporate Gifts and Contributions:* U.S. Treasury Department, *Statistics of Corporate Income Tax Returns,* various years.

APPENDIX TABLE II   After-Tax Income of Corporations Reporting Net Incomes
(Dollar values in millions)

Year	Net Income After Taxes, After Gifts and Contributions[a]		Net After-Tax Cost of Gifts and Contributions		Net Income After Taxes, Before Gifts and Contributions[b]	
	Current Dollars	1936 Dollars	Current Dollars	1936 Dollars	Current Dollars	1936 Dollars
1936	$ 8,571	$ 8,571	$ 23	$ 23	$ 8,594	$ 8,594
1937	8,611	8,264	25	24	8,636	8,288
1938	5,907	5,746	19	18	5,926	5,765
1939	7,842	7,749	23	23	7,865	7,772
1940	8,917	8,674	22	21	8,939	8,696
1941	11,211	10,146	18	16	11,229	10,162
1942	12,155	9,795	31	25	12,186	9,820
1943	13,159	9,894	44	33	13,203	9,927
1944	12,566	9,219	68	40	12,634	9,269
1945	11,668	8,346	89	50	11,757	8,410
1946	18,672	11,954	131	64	18,803	12,038
1947	22,817	13,061	148	84	22,965	13,145
1948	24,788	13,298	146	85	24,934	13,377
1949	21,219	11,457	136	73	21,355	11,531
1950	27,459	14,621	100	53	27,559	14,675
1951	24,124	12,032	113	56	24,237	12,088
1952	22,192	10,831	143	70	22,335	10,900
1953	22,904	11,075	177	86	23,084	11,162
1954	23,822	11,355	148	71	23,970	11,425
1955	30,010	14,096	197	93	30,207	14,188
1956	30,308	13,770	198	90	30,506	13,860
1957	29,667	12,995	198	87	29,865	13,081
1958	26,404	11,274	184	79	26,588	11,353
1959	31,114	13,079	227	95	31,341	13,174
1960	30,685	12,685	228	94	30,913	12,779
1961	32,781	13,380	242	99	33,023	13,479
1962	35,883	14,498	283	114	36,166	14,613
1963	39,208	15,633	312	124	39,520	15,758
1964	45,800	17,961	362	142	46,162	18,103

SOURCE: *Corporation Net Income:* U.S. Treasury Department, *Statistics of Income, Corporate Income Tax Returns,* various years.

[a] Net taxable income, plus income from tax-exempt securities, minus income and excess-profits taxes, plus foreign tax credit. Includes investment credit in years 1962–1964.

[b] Net income after taxes, after gifts and contributions, plus net after-tax cost of gifts and contributions.

APPENDIX TABLE III   Gifts and Contributions as Percentage of After-Tax Income, Corporations Reporting Net Income
(Dollar values in millions)

Year	Gifts and Contributions		Gifts and Contributions as Percentage of Income After Taxes:		Net Income Before Taxes[a]	
	Current Dollars	*1936 Dollars*	*After Gifts and Con- tributions*	*Before Gifts and Con- tributions*	*Current Dollars*	*1936 Dollars*
1936	$ 27	$ 27.0	0.3150	.3142	$ 9,726	$ 9,726
1937	29	27.8	0.3368	.3358	9,848	9,451
1938	23	22.4	0.3894	.3881	6,725	6,542
1939	29	28.7	0.3698	.3687	9,028	8,921
1940	37	36.0	0.4149	.4139	11,406	11,095
1941	57	51.6	0.5084	.5076	18,316	16,576
1942	96	77.4	0.7878	.7878	24,343	19,616
1943	158	118.8	1.2007	1.1967	29,005	21,808
1944	233	170.9	1.8542	1.8442	27,357	20,071
1945	263	188.1	2.2540	2.2370	22,367	15,999
1946	211	135.1	1.1300	1.1222	27,385	17,532
1947	238	136.2	1.0431	1.0364	33,568	19,215
1948	236	126.6	0.9521	0.9465	36,430	19,544
1949	220	118.8	1.0368	1.0302	30,766	16,612
1950	250	133.1	0.9104	0.9071	44,356	23,619
1951	341	170.1	1.4135	1.4069	45,581	22,734
1952	396	193.3	1.7844	1.7730	40,705	19,866
1953	491	237.4	2.1437	2.1270	42,131	20,373
1954	309	147.3	1.2971	1.2891	39,957	19,045
1955	410	192.6	1.3662	1.3573	50,792	23,857
1956	413	187.6	1.3627	1.3538	50,674	23,023
1957	412	180.5	1.3887	1.3795	49,196	21,549
1958	383	163.5	1.4505	1.4405	44,148	18,851
1959	472	198.4	1.5170	1.5060	52,460	22,051
1960	475	196.4	1.5480	1.5366	51,327	21,218
1961	505	206.1	1.5405	1.5292	53,479	21,828
1962	590	238.4	1.6442	1.6314	57,416	23,198
1963	651	259.6	1.6604	1.6473	62,474	24,910
1964	723	283.5	1.5786	1.5662	70,094	27,488

[a] Net taxable income plus income from tax-exempt securities.

APPENDIX TABLE IV Gifts and Contributions, Deficit, and Number
of Corporations Reporting No Net Income
(Dollar values in millions)

| Year | Gifts and Contributions | | Reported Deficit | | Number of Corporations Reporting Deficit (*Thousands*) |
	Amount, Current Dollars	Percentage of Total Corporate Contributions	Current Dollars	Percentage of Reported After-Tax Profit, Net Income Corporations	
1936	$ 3	10.0	$1,707	19.86	276
1937	4	12.1	1,805	20.90	286
1938	4	14.8	2,395	40.42	301
1939	2	6.5	1,649	20.97	270
1940	1	2.6	1,855	20.75	252
1941	1	1.7	1,436	12.79	204
1942	2	2.0	663	5.44	173
1943	1	0.6	592	4.48	137
1944	1	0.4	577	4.57	124
1945	3	1.1	820	6.97	118
1946	3	1.4	1,786	9.50	132
1947	3	1.2	1,766	7.69	169
1948	3	1.3	1,685	6.76	198
1949	3	1.3	2,190	10.26	230
1950	2	0.8	1,310	4.75	203
1951	2	0.6	1,533	6.33	213
1952	3	0.8	1,697	7.60	229
1953	4	0.8	2,068	8.96	256
1954	5	1.6	2,852	11.90	282
1955	5	1.2	2,380	7.88	294
1956	5	1.2	2,771	9.08	326
1957	5	1.2	3,591	12.02	367
1958	12	3.0	4,266	16.04	379
1959	10	2.1	3,996	12.75	404
1960	7	1.5	5,833	18.87	470
1961	7	1.4	5,367	16.25	475
1962	5	0.8	5,406	14.95	485
1963	6	0.9	5,574	14.10	515
1964	6	0.8	5,601	12.13	515

SOURCE: U.S. Treasury Department, *Statistics of Income, Corporation Income Tax Returns,* various years.

APPENDIX TABLE V   Estimated Net After-Tax Cost or "Price" of $1 in Contributions, Corporations with Net Income
(Dollar values in millions)

| Year | Net Income of Corporations That Were: | | Complement of Maximum Marginal Tax Rate | | After-Tax Cost or "Price" of $1 in Contributions |
	Subject to Excess-Profits-Tax Liability	Not Subject to Excess-Profits-Tax Liability	Combined, Normal, Surtax and Excess-Profits Tax	Normal and Surtax Only	
1936	—	—	—	0.85	$ .850
1937	—	—	—	0.85	.850
1938	—	—	—	0.81	.810
1939	—	—	—	0.81	.810
1940	$ 3,920	$ 7,283	0.26	0.76	.585
1941	11,109	7,002	0.09	0.69	.322
1942	17,475	6,577	0.20	0.60	.323
1943	22,751	5,967	0.20	0.60	.283
1944	21,044	6,080	0.20	0.60	.290
1945	14,645	7,520	0.20	0.60	.336
1946	—	—	—	0.62	.620
1947	—	—	—	0.62	.620
1948	—	—	—	0.62	.620
1949	—	—	—	0.62	.620
1950	26,858	17,283	0.28	0.58	.398
1951	24,946	20,387	0.1925	0.4925	.327
1952	16,813	23,619	0.18	0.48	.355
1953	16,793	25,026	0.18	0.48	.360
1954	—	—	—	0.48	.480
1955	—	—	—	0.48	.480
1956	—	—	—	0.48	.480
1957	—	—	—	0.48	.480
1958	—	—	—	0.48	.480
1959	—	—	—	0.48	.480
1960	—	—	—	0.48	.480
1961	—	—	—	0.48	.480
1962	—	—	—	0.48	.480
1963	—	—	—	0.48	.480
1964	—	—	—	0.50	.500

APPENDIX TABLE VI   Estimated Net After-Tax Cost of Reported Gifts and
Contributions, and Net Cost as Percentage of After-Tax
Income, Net-Income Corporations
(Dollar values in millions)

Year	Gifts and Contributions (Current dollars)	"Price" of $1 in Contributions	Net After-Tax Cost of Reported Contributions		Net Income, After Taxes, Before Gifts and Contributions (Current dollars)	Net After-Tax Cost as Percentage of Net After-Tax Income
			Current Dollars	1936 Dollars		
1936	$ 27	$0.850	$ 23	$ 23	$ 8,594	0.27
1937	29	0.850	25	24	8,636	0.29
1938	23	0.810	19	18	5,926	0.31
1939	29	0.810	23	23	7,865	0.30
1940	37	0.585	22	21	8,939	0.24
1941	57	0.322	18	16	11,229	0.16
1942	96	0.323	31	25	12,186	0.25
1943	158	0.283	44	33	13,203	0.33
1944	233	0.290	68	40	12,634	0.43
1945	263	0.336	89	50	11,757	0.59
1946	211	0.620	131	64	18,803	0.53
1947	238	0.620	148	84	22,965	0.64
1948	236	0.620	146	85	24,934	0.64
1949	220	0.620	136	73	21,355	0.63
1950	250	0.398	100	53	27,551	0.36
1951	341	0.327	113	56	24,237	0.46
1952	396	0.355	143	70	22,335	0.64
1953	491	0.360	177	86	23,081	0.77
1954	309	0.480	148	71	23,970	0.62
1955	410	0.480	197	93	30,207	0.66
1956	413	0.480	198	90	30,506	0.65
1957	412	0.480	198	87	29,865	0.67
1958	383	0.480	184	79	26,588	0.70
1959	472	0.480	227	95	31,341	0.72
1960	475	0.480	228	94	30,913	0.74
1961	505	0.480	242	99	33,023	0.73
1962	590	0.480	283	114	36,166	0.78
1963	651	0.480	312	124	39,520	0.79
1964	723	0.500	362	142	46,162	0.78

Appendix B Illustrative Computation of Net After-Tax Cost of Corporate Contributions

APPENDIX TABLE VII   Illustrative Computation of Average Net After-Cost or "Price" of $1 in Corporate Contributions, 1953

Net Income Class	Net Cost of $1 in Contributions	Total Net Income (Deficit) (Millions)	Total Gifts and Contributions (Thousands)
Zero or negative net income	$1.00	($ 2,335)	$ 3,880
Positive net income			
$0 to $25,000	0.70	2,296	
$25,000 and over			490,637
No excess-profits tax	0.48	22,731	
Excess-profits tax	0.18	16,793	

Method of computing average net cost of contributions for corporations with net income

Weight (income)		"Price"		Product
$25,027	×	0.48	=	$12,012
16,793	×	0.18	=	3,023
$41,820				$15,035

$$\text{Average "Price"} = \frac{\$15,035}{\$41,820} = .360$$

ASSUMPTIONS:

1. Corporations with net income of less than $25,000 gave the same percentage of income as those with incomes greater than $25,000 but not in the excess-profits category. This, even though "price" of giving is much higher for the former group. The justification is that corporations with less than $25,000 in net income accounted for a sufficiently small percentage of contributions and income that differences in giving rates would have negligible effect on the average. In the period 1950 to 1963, these under-$25,000 corporations accounted for between 4.9 and 7.3 per cent of the total net income of corporations with net income.

2. Corporations liable for the excess-profits tax gave the same percentage of income as those liable only for the ordinary corporate income tax. This, even though the "price" of giving was much lower for the excess-profits-tax group. This assumption surely leads to an overstatement in the average "price" in those years when the excess-profits tax applied to corporations accounting for a large percentage of corporate net income. In 1953, for example, this assumes that, of the $491 million in contributions made by corporations with a net income, $197 million or only 40 per cent was made by corporations liable for excess-profits taxes, as this was their share of corporate net income.

APPENDIX TABLE VIII   Estimate of Hypothetical 1963 Contributions by
Corporations on the Assumption of the Same Net After-Tax
Percentage of Income That Was Given in 1936–1939
(Dollar values in millions)

	Actual, 1936–39 Average	*Actual, 1963*	*Hypothetical, 1963, Assuming Same Net After-Tax Sacrifice of 1936–39*
Corporations with Net Income			
1. Net income before taxes (1936 dollars)	$8,660	$24,910	$24,910
2. Net income after taxes, after gifts and contributions (1936 dollars)	7,583	15,633	15,712
3. Gifts and contributions (1936 dollars)	26.5	259.6	95.8
4. Net after-tax cost of $1 in giving	0.83	0.48	0.48
5. Net after-tax cost of gifts and contributions (1936 dollars) (3) × (4)	22	125	46
6. Net income after taxes but before gifts and contributions (1936 dollars) (2) + (5)	7,605	15,758	15,758
7. Net after-tax cost of gifts and contributions as percentage of net income after taxes but before gifts and contributions (5) ÷ (6)	0.29	0.79	0.29
Gifts and contributions, 1963 dollars (3) × 2.508		651	240
Add: Contributions of corporations with no net income		6	6
		657	246

Appendix C Regression
Coefficients Relating Corporation
Giving to Successively Larger
Numbers of Explanatory
Variables, Based on Time-
Series Data (Data, logarithmically
transformed, are for the period
1936–1963; T-ratios given in
parentheses)

APPENDIX TABLE IX Scale Elasticity Coefficients

Constant Term	Scale Variables Log₁₀Y	Scale Variables Log₁₀Y_{t-1}	Price Variables Log₁₀P	Price Variables Log₁₀P_{t-1}	Tax-Change Expectations E	Trend T	Adjusted R-Squared	Von Neumann Ratio
−7.52	2.37 (6.26)						0.60	1.07
−2.33	1.01 (1.83)					0.022 (3.07)	0.70	0.59
−0.13	0.82 (1.98)		−0.85 (4.52)			0.021 (4.06)	0.83	0.71
−0.66	1.05 (3.83)			−1.03 (8.63)		0.016 (4.57)	0.93	2.07
−1.19	1.13 (4.31)		0.28 (1.24)	−1.22 (6.18)	0.08 (2.33)	0.012 (4.47)	0.94	1.79
−2.44	0.97 (3.65)	0.46 (1.72)	0.34 (1.58)	−1.26 (6.59)	0.08 (2.44)	0.012 (3.32)	0.94	1.93

APPENDIX TABLE X Profitability Elasticity Coefficients

Constant Term	Income Variables Log₁₀Y	Income Variables Log₁₀Y_{t-1}	Net Worth Log₁₀NW	Price Variables Log₁₀P	Price Variables Log₁₀P_{t-1}	Trend T	Adjusted R-Squared	Von Neumann Ratio
−8.78	2.20 (4.58)		0.39 (0.61)				0.59	1.02
12.35	0.51 (1.06)		−2.57 (3.44)			0.048 (4.99)	0.79	1.08
13.42	0.36 (1.22)		−2.39 (5.23)	−0.81 (6.28)		0.046 (7.76)	0.92	1.20
6.01	0.81 (3.17)		−1.20 (2.81)		−0.90 (7.86)	0.029 (5.24)	0.94	2.64
8.17	0.67 (2.55)		−1.52 (3.29)	−0.29 (1.55)	−0.65 (3.29)	0.034 (5.50)	0.95	2.25
7.83	0.66 (2.46)	0.04 (0.14)	−1.48 (2.68)	−0.28 (1.30)	−0.66 (2.99)	0.033 (4.03)	0.94	2.26

APPENDIX TABLE XI Price Elasticity Coefficients

Constant Term	Price Variables $Log_{10}P$	Price Variables $Log_{10}P_{t-1}$	Scale Variables $Log_{10}Y$	Scale Variables $Log_{10}Y_{t-1}$	Net Worth $Log_{10}NW$	Tax-Change Expectations	Trend T	Adjusted R-Squared	Von Neumann Ratio
4.05	−1.17 (2.98)							0.23	0.22
4.50		−1.43 (4.46)						0.42	0.46
4.48	0.03 (0.06)	−1.46 (2.79)						0.40	0.48
3.12	−0.89 (4.49)						0.030 (8.84)	0.81	0.50
3.41		−1.03 (6.85)					0.027 (9.99)	0.88	1.52
3.47	−0.15 (0.62)	−0.91 (3.81)					0.027 (9.88)	0.88	1.33
3.31	0.06 (0.20)	−1.06 (4.05)				0.06 (1.31)	0.027 (9.97)	0.88	0.93
−0.75		−1.03 (9.08)	1.05 (4.08)			0.06 (1.96)	0.016 (4.83)	0.93	1.48
−1.19	0.28 (1.24)	−1.22 (6.18)	1.13 (4.31)			0.08 (2.33)	0.015 (4.47)	0.94	1.79
−2.44	0.34 (1.58)	−1.26 (6.59)	0.97 (3.65)	0.46 (1.72)		0.08 (2.44)	0.012 (3.32)	0.94	1.93
6.01		−0.90 (7.86)	0.81 (3.17)		−1.20 (2.81)		0.029 (5.24)	0.94	2.64
8.17	−0.29 (1.55)	−0.65 (3.29)	0.67 (2.55)		−1.52 (3.29)		0.034 (5.50)	0.95	2.25

APPENDIX TABLE XII Other Time-Related Factors (Trend Coefficients)[a]

Constant Term	Trend T	Price Variables $Log_{10}P$	$Log_{10}P_{t-1}$	Scale Variables $Log_{10}Y$	$Log_{10}Y_{t-1}$	Tax-Change Expectations	Adjusted R-Squared	Von Neumann Ratio
3.41	0.027 (9.99)		-1.03 (6.85)				0.88	1.52
-0.66	0.016 (4.57)		-1.03 (8.63)	1.05 (3.83)			0.93	2.07
-0.75	0.016 (4.83)		-1.03 (9.08)	1.05 (4.08)	0.06 (1.96)		0.93	1.48
-1.19	0.012 (4.47)	0.28 (1.24)	-1.22 (6.18)	1.13 (4.31)		0.08 (2.33)	0.94	1.79
-2.44	0.012 (3.32)	0.34 (1.58)	-1.26 (6.59)	0.97 (3.65)	0.46 (1.72)	0.08 (2.44)	0.94	1.93

						Net Worth $Log_{10}NW$		
6.01	0.029 (5.24)		-0.90 (7.86)	0.81 (3.17)		-1.20 (2.81)	0.94	2.64
8.17	0.034 (5.54)	-0.29 (1.55)	-0.65 (3.29)	0.67 (2.55)		-1.52 (3.29)	0.95	2.25
7.83	0.033 (4.03)	-0.28 (1.30)	-0.66 (2.99)	0.66 (2.46)	0.04 (0.14)	-1.48 (2.68)	0.94	2.26

[a] Includes only equations with Von Neumann ratios between 1.44 and 2.71. Serial correlation at the 5-per-cent level of significance is indicated if ratio falls outside this range.

APPENDIX TABLE XIII Matrix of Simple Correlation Coefficients for Regressions Based on Time-Series Data, Presented in Appendix Tables IX through XII

| | Gifts and Contributions (log_{10}) X_1 | After-Tax Income (Scale) | | "Price" | | Net Worth Current Year (log_{10}) X_6 | Tax-Change Expectations X_7 | Trend X_8 |
		Current Year (log_{10}) X_2	Preceding Year (log_{10}) X_3	Current Year (log_{10}) X_4	Preceding Year (log_{10}) X_5			
X_1	1.000							
X_2	+.781	1.000						
X_3	+.770	+.772	1.000					
X_4	−.513	−.194	−.268	1.000				
X_5	−.666	−.210	−.263	+.778	1.000			
X_6	+.530	+.600	+.548	−.097	−.046	1.000		
X_7	+.112	−.008	+.068	−.373	−.034	+.080	1.000	
X_8	+.826	+.804	+.794	−.165	−.272	+.860	0.000	1.000

Appendix D

APPENDIX TABLE XIV Matrix of Simple Correlation Coefficients for Regression Equations Based on Cross-Sectional Data, Presented in Text Table 14

	Contri-butions Log_{10} X_1	Number of Corporations Log_{10} X_2	Pre-Tax Profits Log_{10} X_3	Net Worth Log_{10} X_4	Employ-ment Log_{10} X_5	Officers' Compensation Log_{10} X_6	Dividends Log_{10} X_7	After-Tax Profits Log_{10} X_8
X_1	1.000							
X_2	+.516	1.000						
X_3	+.776	+.428	1.000					
X_4	+.740	+.420	+.903	1.000				
X_5	+.680	+.637	+.657	+.664	1.000			
X_6	+.477	+.843	+.615	+.672	+.644	1.000		
X_7	+.854	+.286	+.871	+.885	+.597	+.455	1.000	
X_8	+.818	+.411	+.921	+.950	+.669	+.620	+.955	1.000

Appendix E   Comparison of Nelson and Schwartz Analyses of the Determinants of the Growth in Corporate Giving

A STATISTICAL examination of the income and price elasticities of giving has been made by Mr. Robert A. Schwartz as part of a doctoral dissertation at Columbia University.* Mr. Schwartz uses the same general approach, draws data from the same sources, and covers roughly the same time period as the present study. His analysis differs in significant respects from the present one, however, with important differences in findings. The two studies will here be compared to examine the effects of the two approaches and to determine which one might be regarded as providing more valid interpretation of the historical record.

The Giving and Income Variables

As shown in Appendix Table XV, the measure of giving or income adopted by Schwartz is the average per corporation, profit and loss corporations combined. The measure adopted by Nelson is the aggregate giving or income of all profit corporations taken as a group. An examination of time patterns in the several series led Nelson to the conclusion that the correlation measures would be more directly indicative of the effects being measured, and contain less statistical "static," if the aggregate measures were used.

For one thing, the measure based on averages provides an ambiguous description of how the size of the typical corporate giver has changed over time. One source of this ambiguity is the year-to-year

---
* "Private Philanthropic Contributions—An Economic Analysis," 1966. Schwartz's chapter on corporation giving has been revised and published as "Corporate Philanthropic Contributions," *Journal of Finance*, June, 1968, pp. 479–497. The statistical results are unchanged from those presented in the dissertation and examined here.

APPENDIX TABLE XV   Comparison of Nelson and Schwartz Analyses of the Determinants of the Growth in Corporate Giving

	Nelson	*Schwartz*
Time period covered	1936–1963	1936–1961
Treatment of income variable	Aggregate after-tax income of corporations with net income, deflated for price level changes	Average after-tax income per corporation, profit and loss corporations combined, deflated for price level changes
Treatment of "price" variable	Complement of marginal tax rate, corporations with net income; in excess-profits tax years, weighted average of complements of normal and excess-profits tax marginal rates	Complement of average tax rate, for net income corporations, averaged with price of 100% for loss corporations
Treatment of giving variable	Aggregate gifts and contributions of corporations with net income, deflated for price level changes	Average gifts and contributions per corporation, profit and loss corporations combined, deflated for price level changes

changes in the total number of corporations. Such changes mainly reflect the creation and dissolution of large numbers of small corporations, and reflect "demographic behavior" unrelated to movements in giving. These incidental population changes, for present purposes the equivalent of statistical errors, serve more to obscure the underlying income-giving relationship than to illuminate it.

Based on data expressed on an average per corporation, the Schwartz study found a negative secular trend in both the income and giving series. The decline probably reflects, in the main, the proliferation of small corporations over the period, and not a shift in the size distribution among the larger corporations that account for the preponderance of contributions.

The present study uses data for corporations with net incomes only. The Schwartz study used data for all corporations, including those reporting losses. Examination of the detailed data indicated that the inclusion of loss corporations would introduce spurious short-term and secular movements into the data, and would be especially troublesome in interpreting analyses based on averages. While accounting for less than 2 per cent of total contributions, the relative effect of loss corporations on other magnitudes was much greater. From 1940 through 1963, they ranged from 27 to 53 per cent of the number of corporations in a given year, and offset the income of profitable corporations by total loss that ranged from 4 to 21 per cent of total positive income. (*See Chart C* in *Chapter 2.*) The trend in loss offset contributed to the decline in average income observed in the Schwartz data, rising from an average of 6.1 per cent in 1940–1945 to 16.0 per cent in 1960–1963.

The "Price" Variable

The net after-tax cost of a given amount of contributions is determined by the marginal tax rate to which the corporation is subject. As explained in Chapter 3, contributions are thus made at one of several "prices," depending on the tax status of the corporation. Ideally, the price index would be computed as weighted average of the several prices, each weighted by the amount of contributions made at each price. Unfortunately the data are not classified in a manner which would permit this.

The Nelson price variable retains the marginal tax-rate basis for evaluation, while using a weighting system based on the income of corporations subject to the several tax rates. As explained in Appendix Table VII, this treatment understates, probably to a minor degree, movements in the effective "price" of giving. The Schwartz price variable is based on the average tax rate and, as such, substantially understates the movement in the effective "price" of giving, particularly during periods when the excess-profits tax was faced by changing numbers of corporations.

The differing treatments by Nelson and Schwartz produce significantly different measures of income and price elasticity. A regression, using logarithmically (base 10) transformed variables was run which, except for a slight difference in the time period covered and the addition of a trend variable, reproduced the relevant one presented by Schwartz. A comparison of the two sets of elasticities is presented in tabular form below:

	Income		*Price*	
	Nelson	*Schwartz*	*Nelson*	*Schwartz*
Measure of elasticity	+0.80	+0.63	−0.89	−2.00
Variance in explanatory variable	.0104	.0169	.0199	.0079

The lower measure of income elasticity produced by Schwartz reflects the greater variance in his income variable. As mentioned above, this in turn reflects the spuriously high variability introduced into the income variable by expressing income on a per-corporation basis. Changes in the business population, largely unrelated to giving behavior, thus become a factor serving to reduce the measure of income elasticity.

The high price elasticity found by Schwartz (−2.00) reflects the low variance in his price variable, because, as would be expected, the average tax rate showed much lower variability than the marginal tax rate. The higher variance in the Nelson price variable, on the other hand, produced a lower measure of price elasticity. The influence of tax rates on giving, while appreciable, probably did not demonstrate the degree of short-run responsiveness implied by the very high elasticity coefficients presented in the Schwartz analysis.

Finally, the Schwartz analysis found no relationship between giving and time-related factors other than income and price. This result could have been predicted, given the fact that both per-corporation income and giving showed flat to slightly declining time patterns over the period. But, as shown above, much of the flatness in trend can be attributed to the effect on the averages of loss corporations, a group accounting for only a minute share of giving. Were only profit corporations included in the analysis—and with some adjustment for effects of population changes among small corporations—the Schwartz analysis might well have found (as did the Nelson analysis) that time-related factors other than income and price made a significant separate contribution to the growth in giving.

Appendix F

APPENDIX TABLE XVI The Contributions Dollar

	1965 540 Companies		1962 465 Companies		1959 280 Companies		1955ᵃ 180 Companies		1947 71 Companies	
	Thousands of Dollars	% of Total	Thousands of Dollars	% of Total	Thousands of Dollars	% of Total	Thousands of Dollars	% of Total	Thousands of Dollars	% of Total
Health and welfare										
Federated drives: United Funds and the like	50,558	24.2	39,280	25.5	25,450	25.1	8,378	21.9	6,118	38.0
National health agencies (not included above)	3,176	1.5	2,183	1.4	1,520	1.5	497	1.3	—	—
National welfare agencies (not included above)	4,043	1.9	4,114	2.7	3,340	3.3			—	—
Hospitals										
Capital grants	17,172	8.2	9,369	6.1	9,330	9.2	3,290	8.6	2,093	13.0
Operating grants	2,018	1.0	1,016	0.7	1,410	1.4	—	—	—	—
Other local health and welfare agencies	5,301	2.5	5,140	3.3	2,830	2.8	—	—	—	—
Capital grants (excluding hospitals)	4,653	2.2	2,002	1.2	1,820	1.8	—	—	—	—
TOTAL	86,921	41.5	63,104	40.9	45,700	45.1	19,397	50.7	10,626	66.0
Education										
Higher education										
Scholarships	10,569	5.0	7,832	5.1	4,860	4.8	1,071	2.8	—	—
Fellowships	4,715	2.3	4,271	2.8	4,050	4.0	994	2.6	—	—
Research grants (not treated as a business expense)	5,073	2.4	4,040	2.6	3,440	3.4	1,262	3.3	—	—
Capital funds	15,180	7.3	9,695	6.3	9,930	9.8	2,257	5.9	—	—
Direct unrestricted grants	20,487	9.8	18,813	12.2	8,010	7.9	2,027	5.3	—	—
Grants to state, area and national fund-raising groups	7,068	3.4	4,791	3.1	2,830	2.8	573	1.5	—	—

	Dollars	%	Dollars	%	Dollars	%	Dollars	%	Dollars	%
Education-related agencies	3,741	1.8	1,793	1.2	1,310	1.3	—	—	—	—
Other	8,513	4.1	9,740	6.3	3,340	3.3	3,596	9.4	—	—
Secondary education Capital grants	765	0.4	537	0.3	100	0.1	191	0.5	—	—
Other	4,233	2.0	3,019	2.0	1,720	1.7	—	—	—	—
TOTAL	80,344	38.4	64,531	41.9	39,590	39.1	11,975	31.3	2,254	14.0
Culture (cultural centers, performing arts, museums, etc.)b Operating funds	3,332	1.6					—	—		
Capital grants	2,501	1.2					—	—		
TOTAL	5,833	2.8					1,224	3.2	—	—
Civic causes (municipal and community improvement, good government and the like) TOTAL	12,099	5.8	8,239	5.3	2,940	2.9	—	—	—	—
Other Religious causes	1,053	0.5	589	0.4	400	0.4	191	0.5	—	—
Groups devoted solely to economic education	1,788	0.9	1,756	1.1	1,520	1.5	803	2.1	—	—
Groups in U.S. whose principal objective is aid to other countries	7,868	3.8	2,726	1.8	500	0.5	114	0.3	—	—
Causes other than above	8,474	4.0	10,856	7.1	7,200	7.1	1,759	4.6	—	—
TOTAL	19,183	9.2	15,927	10.3	9,630	9.5	2,869	7.5	3,220	20.0
Dollars not identifiable because donee is unknown	4,916	2.3	2,341	1.5	3,540	3.5	2,792	7.3	—	—
GRAND TOTAL	209,296	100.0	154,142	100.0	101,400	100.0	38,260	100.0	16,100	100.0

NOTE: Summary worksheets supplied by John H. Watson III, Manager of Company Contributions, National Industrial Conference Board.
a The breakdown of the contributions dollar for the years 1947 and 1955 was less refined than for subsequent years. As a consequence, distribution of gifts within major areas of support is incomplete.
b Culture and Civic Causes were not tabulated separately prior to 1965.

INDEX